Candles at Home

My

Schizoaffective

Disorder

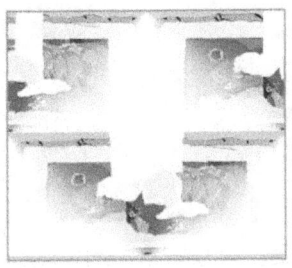

Stella Grey

Life Story,

Art and

Poetry

by,

Stella Grey

This book is

dedicated to my

mother, my

father...

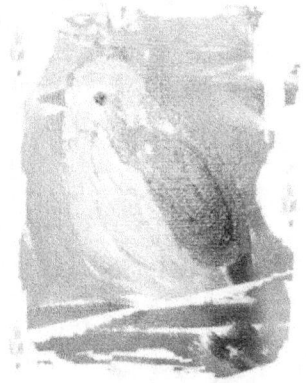

and

Mental Health

Staff

TABLE OF CONTENTS

INTRODUCTION

During my years of having schizoaffective disorder[1], I have experienced instances of complete normalcy. At this same time, I have also suffered from several concurrent afflictions including: disorganized thinking, paranoia, delusions, clinical depression, and panic attacks. I was diagnosed as the "manic type" which, additionally, causes me to sometimes experience extreme highs and lows. My grandmother on my mother's side was a full-blown schizophrenic and that is most likely how I inherited the gene. I was not diagnosed with full-blown schizophrenia, but this specific disorder that I was born with: a relative of or, some say a form of schizophrenia has been, as it is for all schizophrenics who suffer from this illness, quite a hindrance. I am also blessed to be born artistically talented, and thankfully, with very gifted creative and intelligent parents. They have understood me and guided me all of my life.

My journey has not been easy, although I am lucky to be viewed by the outside world, much of the time, as being normal now. I have never thought of hurting others or myself. My secret is that I am actually very conflicted. I am sharing my reality so that others can understand more fully what schizophrenia and schizoaffective disorder really are. Schizoaffective disorder actually has some unique characteristics of it's own, which I will explain more fully in this book.

In the media and among most people I meet there seems to be a major misunderstanding about schizophrenia. As a result, a stigma has been created that affects me as well as other schizophrenics: in particular, the prevalent belief that we are all dangerous. It is very important to note that this popular myth is *definitely* and most often, not true. To the contrary, almost all

---

[1] Schizoaffective disorder is a condition in which there are disturbances in thinking, feeling and relating (Bernhiem. Lewine 1979) Some experts say it is a less extreme form of schizophrenia, while others think it is entirely separate..

7

schizophrenics are introverted and are not at all dangerous. For example, can you imagine my shock when I – for all my life a very non-violent person, was diagnosed with a form of this disorder in 1993? Hearing that word "about me" after the way I had often seen schizophrenics portrayed in movies and on television, I was more nervous and afraid about that specific misconception than I was of anything else.

I was 25 years old when I finally began to strongly suspect that something could possibly be wrong with me. At the time, I was also in an unhappy relationship and had begun to find myself more frequently taking a journey into a different world - a world of my own inner mind and inner dialect. I believe now that I was actually doing this in order to escape clinical depression. It had seemed like just a game to me, at first. What I didn't know at the time was that it all would later turn into a complete downfall for me - and then to indignation later on. Although, at the onset of my disorder, I had still managed to hold jobs, while silently talking to myself and believing spirits were listening to my thoughts, my disease worsened quickly. It would eventually result in a complete lack of self-confidence on my part and in my increased inability to even socialize or to work.

By this time, I had already found my "inner world" or "inner dialect" to be very compelling and, as a result, I stayed quiet most of the time. My brain was created that way and I was actually becoming a slave to those coping mechanisms, progressively trapped in my own inner world. My mind has the will to do what will comfort it the most, in that particular manner, and at the same time continue to still work, function and maintain a somewhat normal facade. Of course, retreating into my "different world" (inner world) was also causing me to progressively lose some social skills at that same time. I never really did have impressive social skills, but I would gladly take back the few I had before I became so engaged and enveloped in the world that I retreated into at the onset of my symptoms.

My schizoaffective disorder, like schizophrenia, has limited my own life in several ways. I would have gratefully just become a great mom or a decently paid artist. Having as much energy as I have had most of the time, I have felt, above all, that I should have been a highly accomplished workaholic, actively involved in social endeavors and projects. However, my illness also places me isolated, in my own inner world, sometimes in order to just cope and survive. I *have* been able to survive by doing this and, in some ways, to even enjoy my own life up until my present age of 49 years old, which is why I am able to write this book now and to share my journey with you. It has taken courage, but I've made a lot of progress through my own efforts, along with good treatment and carefully prescribed medication, which is a dream come true for those with my disease.

I am not ashamed of my illness anymore. I am now also able to distinguish between what is a fantasy or delusion and what is not. However, my illness still marks my daily life with the persistent occurrence of several different delusions or fantasies that I must continually process. Because of their frequency, I have come to accept that I will always be inner-world related (as opposed to outer-world related and sociable) at any time that my disorder forces me to be. I still panic during most social situations. In addition, I also feel "stupefied" a lot which forces me to escape from certain situations. I now think that these moments happen when my mental balance is being upset. It just becomes very overwhelming for me to socialize sometimes, and when that happens, I would much rather experience the peace and quiet of aloneness. This is why I am not like the rest of the "normal" world. I also think that the medication I take helps me to sort things like this out and to better accept myself.

My father passed away in May, 2007. He was a great person, even though he was an alcoholic. He taught me how to draw and paint and loved me to the ends of the earth. He was also a gifted writer and painter, so it is natural that I would eventually blossom into becoming a writer and painter myself. Moreover, my father always let me know that I was different from the very beginning. He always used to say to me, "You are an Artist!"

Given my own situation and life experience with schizophrenia, I now feel that being told that by him was very reaffirming. Both my mother and my father instilled a sense of pride in me which has given me the tools necessary to keep on going in life.

Since, my mother and father also met as fellow artists and writers, it was no surprise that I was born artistic. My mother, who is still a painter and writer herself was finally diagnosed with acute panic attacks and hypomania, a characteristic of Bipolar 2 disorder[2] in 1990. She always was, and still is, a strong domineering and extremely sharp-witted person who also nurtured my artistic side continually. I mention the importance of my parent's encouragement because, for example, some parents are strict to teach a child to fit in and they constantly remind them, "You are no different from everyone else." That is true, in the sense that everyone should be valued equally, but let's face it we *are all different!* Every human being has something different and important to offer.

My father and mother also both taught me that, even when I am critical of my art projects, I am still an artist and *different in a unique and positive way* from those who are not artists. *This may have* saved my life! Actually, the *real truth* is that Art *has saved my life* - and I often even feel that I have even succeeded at it! My story is a story of hope. It is the hope that I have always had no matter what! I have made it through life, even while growing up with my illness, at first a silent condition for the most part. I have still managed to do many of the things that most people enjoy. Once I actually knew I had the condition and sought the appropriate treatment, my life improved and even changed completely and for the better!

I am *not* different from others in many ways because I have always wanted to do all of the normal things people do, and also to achieve what they want to achieve socially and academically.

---

[2] Bipolar 2 is a similar but less extreme form of bipolar1 with moods cycling between high and low over time. Moods seldom if ever reach full blown mania. These less intense elevated moods in bipolar 2 are called hypomanic episodes. (Web MD, 2015)

I have really struggled when attempting to do this most of the time, but I just keep on pursuing my dreams in life. Some of my relationships with other people have been difficult to maintain. In fact, interactions with others during my childhood years in Pasadena and Port Hueneme, California, my schooling, and three questionable close relationships with others, have all contributed to my eventual alienation from many of the people I have known. My fear of those I do not know, then and now, has also created challenges and taken a big toll on me whenever I have tried to engage myself socially. This was often true even long before I knew that I had schizophrenia.

The greatest triumph for me, especially as a woman, has been just surviving "The FACE" which is a serious and common characteristic of my illness - but also a tortured part of my life - buried deep in my soul. It is a horrible symptom of my disease that manifests itself as an unattractive, twisted distorted facial expression when I try to assert myself. "The FACE" is *very* frightening for me, and it is also humiliating - and it is deeply painful. When it happens, it feels as if all control of my facial muscles has suddenly been lost. This sensation continues for a temporary period of time, and is also accompanied by the feeling that I cannot respond to others. This feeling is what expert professionals refer to as the flat effect.[3] I will be explaining 'The FACE" further in later chapters, as well as many other manifestations of schizoaffective disorder and schizophrenia that I struggle with every day. It is my sincere hope that by sharing my story I will be able to help others by shedding a lot of light on this (my) debilitating disease.

---

[3] The flat effect is a flattening of emotions and the loss of interest in activities that others find pleasurable. (Torrey, 2001)

Believe

I can believe if
I am having a
good day
"The FACE"
approaching
as I listen
to what others
say
others won't see
the inner turmoil
those raging seas
like waves
I would like to
believe
I can still be
saved...

Tulips (2006)

Self portrait 1985

A Joy to be Found   (1988)

CHAPTER ONE

As a Child

My father and mother separated when I was four years old and I stayed with some friends of my father's for almost a year. I didn't really think of it as a traumatic experience when it happened, because I had been devotedly nurtured by them for the years before their break up. I was a happy and well-adjusted child, or at least I thought so, for many years. However, I did have a few bad experiences, early on, that would impact my life forever and I continued searching for those "lost marbles" for a long time. Up until my thirties I also used to bite my nails, like my mother did, and as a result was denied Twinkies as a child. I also remember a more painful incident at the age of five, when I was staying with my father's friends who, before that, had been complete strangers to me. I was there because my grandfather and father had come and taken me from my mother who was living among hippies in San Francisco - a place my grandfather did not approve of.

I remember getting into some marbles that belonged to another child from that family. Then, I swallowed one, by accident, and lied about it. I told my caregivers that I had lost the marble in the backyard and was sent to find it for what seemed like an eternity to me. I still remember that day so clearly. Looking back at my life now, it seems as if I would just keep searching for that lost marble, over and over again, until my thirties. I also remember, one time, at about age four, suddenly getting really excited, then catching a bee in my hand - only to get stung. Life has kind of felt like that to me sometimes, too.

Shortly after that time period, I began staying with my father and his new girlfriend and he made a disturbing comment that I remember to this day. He was watching the news about a kidnapping, when he looked at me with very, very, sad eyes and warned me to watch out because he would never want "this" to happen to me. As a result, I became afraid to walk alone from school. When I got older, I was also scared in many other situations that "this" could happen to me - and, to this day, I fear possible abductors. This would become only one of my many fears as time went on. I was also quite sad at the time, not really because of my father's sadness when he warned me, but for reasons still unknown to me. In addition, I just felt out of place staying with my father and his girlfriend. It was almost as if he had changed. He was also depressed about losing my mother, afraid of losing me, and he had a drinking problem. I wondered why he had wanted me to stay with those strangers and felt confused. I really did not want to stay with him anymore.

It was wonderful when my mother finally came to get me. She had come back for me at last! I can only remember feeling happy and excited to see her, however, all was still not perfect. The new problem was that I wasn't the only child anymore. She arrived with my new baby brother in her arms and, from the beginning, I was jealous of him. He was noisy and there were times when he would stare at me, like babies often do, and it would infuriate me. I would raise my voice in loud rebellion. "He is staring at me!" I would say. Then, in response, or at other times when I rebelled, my mother would sometimes pinch my ear. She was never one to spank us, but she was usually very strict. She did not put up with any talking back or misbehaving and she let us know that early on. One time I got yanked by the arm so hard that I decided to become a good kid just to avoid the consequences of misbehaving.

As a child, I was different from other children and a close observer. I frequently felt estranged or from other kids, so I would keep my distance from them, often playing handball or riding my bicycle alone. I always felt they (other children) must have had more "going" for themselves than I did because I sometimes felt ignored. I also remember taking ballet lessons that were extremely uncomfortable for me. A really scary, mean second grade teacher also made me feel like I wasn't "right" somehow, and I would later have these feelings a lot in my life. Her yoga instructions in class were unbearable and I hated trying to put my body in those positions. I realize now that she was trying her best, in a subtle way, through enforcing yoga exercises, to engage all of her students. Yet, this made me feel really self-conscious and trying to participate was extremely hard for me.

I did have one escape from my early inhibitions on a special occasion, or at least I thought it was one - just for me. When I was seven, my father gave me some coffee at a very nice restaurant when I was visiting him and I was very bubbly and happy afterward. My mother, of course, didn't agree with what he had done. I was way too young to be drinking coffee and was already having trouble sleeping. I often sleepwalked from an early age and would sometimes even wake up in the middle of the night and talk to a wall as if it were a phone. Looking back, I think I may have been feeling the intense pressure around me that my mother was experiencing at the time. She was living in a brief but very volatile relationship, constantly trying to keep a dangerous alcoholic from becoming violent. Thankfully, there were very few actual violent explosions before we left, but the underlying stress in the household was quite intense.

I was also a night eater. I could barely finish my dinner half of the time, but would wake up in the middle of the night, to ask for more food. Finally, after months of this, my mother made me stay at the table, sometimes until 10:00 pm, to finish my dinner! I then discovered ways of trying to trick my mother and would smear some food under the table or around and under the edges of the plate to make it look as if I had eaten more. Again, looking back, perhaps we were living in the middle of a crisis and as a result I felt too uptight to eat. Besides what kid likes eggplant anyway!

One fun experience for me during my childhood was going to Disneyland. I especially liked the ride "Small World" and sometimes, my mother would sing the song from that ride to me.

I also enjoyed going to the movies with my family or friends but I didn't like my supposedly friendly next door neighbors taking me at the tender age of only seven years with them to see "The Exorcist". I crouched and hid in back of the seats at the theater. I've never been so terrified in my life! I still wonder to this day what possessed that family to take me to that movie - the scariest movie of all time and I was way too young to watch that kind of movie. My ceramics class and drama classes were also fun, but more than anything I loved being with my father and, especially, with my adoring grandfather. Unfortunately, I didn't see them very often, though, after I went to live with my mother - especially my grandfather who was upset at the time because my mother was in an interracial relationship. This was the same violent one that brought my younger brother and sister into the world. Sadly, my grandfather died when I was only eight years old and it was so hard for me to believe, a really big shock, because I was barely old enough to understand death.

Eventually, as very little time went by, the same new stepfather my grandfather disliked so much was becoming more dangerous and began threatening my mom. She finally left everything behind, escaped him, and we began a totally new life in the city of Pasadena. My mother, my brother, my new sister and I all stayed for six weeks at a battered women's shelter where my siblings and I played joyfully at first. However, one night I tried to go to sleep there, and I heard marching sounds in my pillow. I was so terrified and my ears were also pounding really hard. I told my mother what was going on and she let me watch television in the living room. Then I began to think that the news lady from the program was popping out of the television set! After six weeks at the shelter, we all started a new life "from scratch", in a small apartment, with nothing to speak of in our new city of Pasadena.

I was eight, my brother was three and my sister was two years old so, for a brief time, we all stayed in day care while my mother worked or went to school. One day my mother found out that I had become the target of a group of bullies at day care. I was uncomfortable and a little scared of my mother's reaction because she seemed quite a bit more startled and disturbed about this than I was. The administration handled the problem that day, and my mother immediately took us all out of day care. As for further incidents of bullying, I was safe from that for a while and adjusted to my new third grade classroom very well.

My life was now still in many ways normal. During my preteen years, I became both a tomboy and a regular girl. I loved skateboarding and once rode a skateboard barefooted in the rain. (This was actually a normal thing to do for a kid living in Pasadena. Even if it was raining there, it was often still warm outside.) I also loved watching "The Bionic Woman", a popular TV show during mid 70's. What I loved about it, I realize now, was that she looked a lot like my mother. I often even dreamed that she *was* my mother. I also used to imagine that Lindsey Wagner (the Bionic Woman) *was inside my thoughts with me* - sometimes nurturing me. I wanted the Bionic Woman Barbie doll for so long and felt sad because we were poor and I couldn't have her. Then, at the age of nine, I finally did get her - after what seemed like an eternity waiting, and I was so happy. She felt so significant to me, at that time, that I slept with her. I loved that Bionic Barbie SO much! I loved her much more than any toy I have ever received before or afterward.

I still missed my father so much and his absence was the most painful part of my childhood and early teenage years. I really saw very little of him, and it seemed as if I was always wishing he was around. Twice a year, I would ride the bus to see him in Long Beach and when I visited him, we would play Monopoly, Frisbee, and some games of pool together at the taverns he often frequented. I realize now that he really helped to build my confidence. He also taught me all about the religion called Scientology, as I became old enough to understand the concepts. Scientology was my father's own answer to life - his saving grace - and I absorbed it like a sponge. During our visits I learned more and more and even visited other Scientologists with him. The concepts had a tremendous impact on me and my father's teachings helped strengthen my confidence even more. Ironically, I would later discover that learning about Scientology would also serve to silence the reality of my illness for a long time to come.

My childhood was sometimes also difficult living with a mother who I now realize had a Bi-Polar 2 condition, PTSD and a panic disorder. I experienced "second-hand" her own frequent highs (feelings of extreme excitement) and her occasional lows (feeling depressed) and I had a lot of the same fears and anxieties that she did. We were also very poor growing up and my mother couldn't afford to take us out very often to show us her fun side. I think that my mother's own problems caused me, and maybe all of us sometimes, to feel too poor, depressed, or even angry. My mother always also seemed so busy, working all of the time to support our family, and when she wasn't working she was involved with her own art or creative projects, new ideas for making money or new businesses. Perhaps because of this, I frequently felt left out, out of place, scared and unwanted.

One day I had experienced enough problems in my life and was feeling extremely angry. Along with my other usual challenges, my personal belongings had begun to disappear at times. On that particular day I could see my very young, mischievous siblings leaving my room from the hallway! I was not only angry at them for sneaking in my room, I was also suspicious and concluded that somehow, in some way, it was really a "plot" they were in against me. In a sense, at this very young age I may have already been experiencing some early symptoms of schizophrenia. I have guilt to this day, for using a belt on my younger brother and sister that day for getting into my things and my sister still has a tiny scar from it. Yet at the same time, it seemed to me as if what very little *I did have* in life was being totally violated.

My depression, and what I believe was the beginning stages of my disease as a kid, definitely also caused me to have poor concentration at school. History bored me, math really challenged me, and other subjects were just too hard for me to

20

grasp. I was so relieved when I could remember all of the states in the U.S.A. or remember a history lesson. I did enjoy recognition by my fifth grade teacher who made the class recite the Pledge of Allegiance every day before lunch. I felt a sense of comfort saying the every school day devotion to my country; it gave me an unexpected sense of belonging. I also began to really excel in art that same year and my artwork was used as an example for the other students. My fifth grade teacher said it was because of my "beautiful use of colors".

My only girlfriend or early real childhood friend, at that time, was a nice girl named Lynn. She was never critical of me and we never fought with each other. We played handball, games, Barbie's, and watched TV together and she also had an adorable cat. I wanted desperately to play with her cat or just to touch it but the cat always got up and turned around when I tried to. It was really unsettling for me that Lynn would smile all the time while petting her cat and that I was so nervous and high-strung that I couldn't do the same. I wondered to myself, "Why did she smile at me like that?" These thoughts really irritated me and made me feel insignificant so I began to hold a grudge against Lynn. Then, hoping to understand our relationship better, I tried to apply the principles of Scientology[4] and evaluate Lynn's emotional tone level in response to what my father had taught me.

I realize now, that I was already beginning to label my friend Lynn unfairly. I also believe now that I shouldn't have been using the religion of Scientology in that way or at that time. Today, as I look back, I also have guilt for resenting and eventually pulling away from her, my only good friend. By the age of twelve, I had ultimately rejected Lynn – completely - for

---

[4] Scientologists often evaluate people using a scale based on their emotions. This was created by L. Ron Hubbard and is called "the tone scale". There are a total of fifteen emotional levels in which individuals exist, "Enthusiasm is the highest; level of functioning. On the lower parts of the scale there are several emotions such as covert hostility, grief and the lowest one is apathy. (Minshull, 1972)

no other valid reason that I can even think of now, except for my own application of Scientology to her, and I deeply regret judging my friend so harshly and disconnecting from her. I would, at times, encounter Lynn, later in life, but it wasn't the same between us anymore. We have not kept in touch, like I once had wanted to do, and I always wonder how things could have been if we were still friends. Lynn had rescued me in the third grade by offering her friendship when I was scared and isolated during my first day of classes. I often wondered how could I have been so uncaring to desert her in the way I did.

As time went on, the longer I lived in Pasadena there seemed to be even more adjustments that I had to make. My mother's new black boyfriend had two teenage daughters and they moved in with us. They were both African American, but Sherry, the younger daughter was close to my age so I could actually relate to her in many ways. As it turned out, I really welcomed the change in our household and was glad to have a distraction from the problems I was having with girls of my own race. Looking back, I don't regret being around so much racial diversity, during my youth, even though it was sometimes confusing to me. I often wondered, for instance, what it meant that I felt more comfortable around Sherry than my own white girlfriends. My mother also seemed happy for me that I was able to get along with Sherry so well - she embraced black culture and as it turned out, I began to do the same.

I appreciated my mother's easy going nature, her open mind, and the support she gave me, yet I still remained conflicted about her. At the time, I also felt somewhat guilty for holding grudges against her, but I was very close with my father and learning about Scientology from him, so I even evaluated and labeled her as an "angry" person on the Scientology "Tone Scale". I did this because I felt that she rejected me one time for bringing what I felt was a positive attitude home from school. She had not felt it was genuine and raised her voice at me. I think I may have also been finding it hard to relate to what I realized later, were her frequent hypomanic states of mind and

22

also her extreme anxiety at certain times. On some occasions, I would avoid her, even when she was nice. I know, on the other hand, that she always nurtured all of us, guided us, and gave us really good advice. Later on, my mother and I would, thankfully, begin to develop real mutual trust and understanding. We even have become close friends. My mother gave me a gold necklace which I still keep and treasure to this day.

CHAPTER TWO

A Beginning and an End

In the seventh grade, my mother took me to get the perfect haircut which really made me feel more confident. My hair had always been long and straight and everyone told me it looked beautiful, but I never liked it. After the perfect haircut, a quiet boy named Juan from school noticed me. We went on a class trip to Magic Mountain together and he rode behind me on one of the rides. This was a turning point in my young life - that a guy, any guy, would want to become friends. I was happy and surprised, however, I soon noticed that Juan was really quiet and I somehow took that as a rejection. I remember feeling for a very long time that my friendship with him had turned out very poorly. Looking back, I now feel it was actually early problems with my own perceptions and how I interpreted social situations.

Soon after my new haircut, I also got a beautiful yellow blouse which I really, really loved. I was now so optimistic and happy because I rarely got new clothes. Juan, Lynn (still my friend at that time), and I all went horseback riding and I was initially thrilled about the new adventure. Riding a horse seemed like heaven to me, at first, until we got there - and my negative reaction occurred immediately, as soon as we arrived. It was actually a disappointment, looking back now. Already at age twelve, I was thinking "This is worthless and I am undesirable anyway." I kept thinking, "Why can't I think this is fun?" I realized much later that a trademark of schizophrenia is dulled emotions or the "flat effect"[5] which I know now I was already feeling on various occasions. Eventually, Juan found another

---

[5] The "flat effect" is described earlier in my Introduction.

girlfriend, then I inwardly criticized myself and Juan as well.

Finally, during that same 7th grade school year, a time still very meaningful for me, what seemed at first to be another real friendship came along. A girl who was very fashionable and also very beautiful now also wanted to be my friend. Her name was Shelly and she approached me as I was picking up my books after lunch. At first glance, I thought she might want to say something terrible to me, so I was apprehensive about our encounter, but instead, Shelley seemed kind. I remember reminding myself at that moment to be confident because I was so nervous and suspicious of others. Scared of being rejected, I thought of my mother who was always self-assured in social endeavors. My mother and I were the "spitting image", visually, of one another, so I actually imagined that I *was* my mother on campus that day! I managed to form a new "identity", smiling and acting as if I were her.

Shelley accepted me and we became the best of friends. We were enthusiastic and happy together. At this time, I had rejected Lynn because I couldn't relate to her anymore and, like many teenagers, I was continually struggling with my identity and sense of self. I knew how to present myself, at times, but would still fall short during conversations and relating to others. I believe now that these serious difficulties were the result of schizophrenia. Added to that, as early as junior high school, "The FACE" would often threaten to physically and biologically infiltrate my facial composure and end my enthusiasm! As my illness progressed, this was the forerunner and source of the problem that ultimately created my complete downfall.[6]

I believe now that this happened and had such a disruptive, negative effect on my young adult years because I actually should have obtained treatment from a real doctor or

---

[6] Described earlier as the "flat effect", this experience caused me to grimace as well so it greatly hindered my social abilities. A grimace is a distortion of the face as if a person were expressing negative emotions such as pain. (Webster's New World dictionary 1990)

psychiatrist early on, instead of just relying upon my father's interpretation of Scientology. Yet, my symptoms at that time were also not yet severe or even dramatically different from the behaviors and insecurities expressed by many teenagers. Those that were more unusual I was pretty successful at keeping secret and hidden from others. Above all, I would never trade the childhood love and respect I had for my father or the counseling I received from him. At the time, talking about art with him, Scientology, and other life lessons he shared with me were extremely valuable and significant to me. In some ways, I am also thankful to have been diagnosed with schizoaffective disorder much later in life, as opposed to earlier in my childhood. I say this because it is generally believed that *the earlier the diagnosis of schizophrenia, the worse the outcome is likely to be.*[7]

Later on in my teenage years, the threat of "The FACE" would ultimately make me very miserable. I was always feeling completely motivated to avoid it, distracted by avoiding it, feeling run down from it, and feeling the pressure more than ever to hide it. I think as "The FACE" stayed hidden, I was also always looking for someone to blame "It" on. My bad memories of being yanked by the arm by my mother made it easy to blame her. I also avoided "The FACE" by always pretending to be enthusiastic, no matter what. "Enthusiasm" is a level of emotion described as "high functioning" in Scientology but, at the same time, it was excruciatingly tiring for me to keep up expressing that "enthused" image. I was taking it to the extreme and expressing enthusiasm, even at inappropriate times, and when it didn't feel natural. I was too young to understand that other emotions like anger were natural, too, not only for Scientologists to experience, but for the entire human race! I just wanted to be enthusiastic all the time - "no matter what". Anger was "bad",

---

[7] Torrey, E. Fuller (2001)

according to my own interpretation.

I also had my own assumptions about Scientology and was judging everyone else on an "Emotional Tone Scale", which is something Scientologists do. I wanted to be different and special from others by never becoming *angry,* and thus hopefully, avoiding "The FACE". The only real credit I can give to my analytical behavior, during that time, is that it kept me from fully judging and confronting *my own emotions* and kept my attention primarily on others. Was doing that helpful? Maybe. Or maybe not. Nonetheless, Scientology and my Dad's preaching, to that extent, seemed to help my confidence, at the time, and it also made me feel really smart. After all, higher emotional tone levels are considered very beneficial by Scientology and also good for your physical health. Having a loving and intelligent father also made me very comfortable with males later on in life. In contrast, the problems I experienced with my mother would multiply as I grew older, along with more problems with other females.

Junior High was exciting. I got a permanent for my hair and others noticed my new attitude. I got elected for a school office and made Head Cheerleader and this was another shockingly pleasant surprise which I owed to my association with Shelley. My new social status felt significant even though it didn't fully develop into as much as I would have wanted it to. I remember going to the school officer meetings, feeling apprehensive and thinking to myself, "Am I going to have to say something?" Luckily I never had to, which also seemed sort of weird to me. Ironically, I would feel a sense of relief, but also a bit of failure that I had not been called upon. I wondered how to accept my "position" and also felt like maybe I had "tricked" everyone. Despite all of this new attention, I still remained quiet and rushed through all of my classes. My mind was so overwhelmed! I was actually "play acting" (role-playing) with a "new attitude" in social situations because, when I "play acted", I was no longer the "ugly duckling" in Junior High School. This behavior has been studied in depth by experts and I gained more personal understanding about it much later through seeking therapy and by reading "Schizophrenia Symptoms Causes Treatments" (Bernheim, Lewine 1979).

In the early stages of my friendship with Shelley, we had a lot of fun. We put on makeup together, went shopping, and to parties and clubs (pretending to be 18 years old). We called love hotlines on the telephone for fun and sunbathed together. There were many sleepovers at Shelley's house, too, as I often begged to spend the night with her. I formed a much more confident identity from my new friendship with her, only to lose it due to teenage rivalry later on. I still remained afraid during that time, however, of what was unknown to me and I was also was still very quiet. My self-esteem was continuing to suffer, in a way, because of social problems *with everyone else* around me. It seemed like every time I tried to socialize I either "blanked out" or some voice in my head suddenly turned me around and stopped me right in my tracks! Yet, despite all of this, I remained hopeful about my "new attitude".

I began to realize that Shelley had somewhat manipulative ways, but I still didn't hold grudges against her. Instead, I turned my frustration inward and eventually began to perceive that my "new attitude" was for some reason being rejected by Shelley! I realize now that this also was due to my progressively crippling disease from an early age. I cursed myself a long time for all of the things I desperately needed to do, but just couldn't. I knew deep down something was wrong with me, but I kept going back to Scientology ethics, theories, and methods for an explanation from a young age and into my early twenties. I truly felt there wouldn't be anything wrong if I just applied Scientology, and that it would save me. I know now that my "blunted" emotions, lack of interest in social stimulation, and extreme lack of concentration even during those somewhat complacent "youthful" times would lead me to later realize that I had been affected by this disease from very early on.

For as long as I can remember, I have also felt extremely distracted and had panicky feelings when trying to engage in any activity for too long. Sadly, I didn't know until later that I had a mental illness. When you don't know that you have something medically or psychologically wrong, it can be even more devastating, just trying to cope with a mystery! I would literally struggle very hard up until the age of 26, never knowing what was wrong with me and never receiving proper therapy and medical treatment! It became a very long, painful journey that eventually built up more and more rage inside me - and then relentlessly tore me down. Some might argue that it was just poor concentration due to depression and even I originally thought this might be true. I also tried to find other reasons for how I felt, other excuses, or any other explanation, but I now know for certain that it was always a lot more than poor self-confidence or depression. It *was* schizophrenia

During my junior high years in Pasadena, my entire family - which included my black stepfather and two stepsisters moved into a big beautiful house surrounded with lots of colorful rose bushes. I already loved parties and my popular stepsisters really knew how to throw them! It was now all about dancing and boys for us. Most of the time I could manage to mingle comfortably with others who were not my race and with Shelley who was mixed-ethnicity Caucasian and Hispanic. Then, when summer vacation arrived and, soon, began to end, my youngest new "stepsister", Sherry, took me shopping to the garment district in Los Angeles for Fall season school clothes. I loved shopping with her, finding clothing bargains with the money I had earned from working at the Summer Youth Employment program.

By the time I entered high school, I began to feel somewhat uneasy about my relationship with Shelley. I thought that maybe, she was acting strange towards me! Then, one morning after a sleepover, she put her head on my shoulder while we were laying down together. It was among our peers a somewhat normal "girlfriend" gesture, but I felt uncomfortable about it. I also felt as if maybe I shouldn't feel that way. Yet, on the other hand, it somehow seemed inappropriate to me and I was very confused. It was very painful for me that I couldn't mentally or emotionally accept and embrace Shelley's unexpected gesture. It actually made me feel a sudden sense of "frenzy." I now know, however, that for those who have schizophrenia the senses are heightened in an often uncomfortable way .[8]

I also began to think that from the way she looked at me, from then on, that something suddenly was going terribly wrong between us. I kept thinking that she was always looking at me funny. I resolved to think that maybe I was just imagining things, but due to my perceptions of her behavior, I began to feel very embarrassed and anxious about our interactions from that point on. I still kept telling myself it was "okay', though, and I also believed that the "nicer" I was, the better life would be for me. Looking back now, I think that Shelley had found a "button to push" on me. She was witty and smart and she *did know* that I was uncomfortable with her "way" of looking at me. *Maybe* she was actually making me feel uncomfortable to keep my attention away from *her own* personal problems and insecurities during that time, so I dismissed a lot of her shortcomings. Rather than assert myself, I just kept making excuses for Shelley - in my eyes, she could do no wrong.

My time with Shelley was also the beginning of my obsessing about many things: beautiful people, clothes, cars, and movie stars. She and I would watch TV together and suddenly, my mind would begin "swarming." I was uncomfortable often around my best friend Shelley, at this point, but I still didn't realize I was slowly losing control - both of myself - and of the relationship with her. Added to this, there were also many instances of "normal" rivalry between her and I right from the start, that made me question myself. I wanted to speak up for myself or assert myself as others normally did, but always mindful and nervous of "The FACE", I never did. I always endured these painful experiences even if I felt demeaned by

---

[8] Since auditory hallucinations represent an awareness of preconscious incorrect interpretation of auditory stimuli they are likely to increase in conditions of ambiguous sensory input. (Cromwell, Snyder 1993)

them. If "The FACE" ever showed itself, it would really humiliate me! At the time, perhaps, speaking up for myself could have saved our friendship.

When Shelley and I started John Muir High School, she suddenly did not want to "hang out" with me at lunch anymore. My new isolation during those lunch breaks was uncomfortable and also shocking to me at the same time after thinking for so long that we were best friends. I felt right back at square one socially - isolated and unwanted again. I still called her on the phone from time to time, and we would both act like "phony people" the same way we had always play-acted together before, but we talked less and less. Looking back, I guess I was "let down easy". I still continued to look up to Shelly though, and couldn't accept the loss of the close friendship we had shared in the beginning. Shelly did help me see beauty in myself and the world around me and I realize now that I had become *obsessed with being like her - and being liked by her*. Shelley and her mom had been like 'gods' to me, at that time in my life, and despite everything else, she had always been there with a willingness to talk and her mother was amazingly accepting of me, too. I had not really looked up to anyone else like I did Shelley and her mom. My father was seldom around and my mother was seemingly detached and busy. At the same time, I was probably in no way able to interpret these things correctly when my mind and perceptions were always failing me.

Reflecting upon all of this now, I realize that during my teen years and even until today, I have always had trouble with the way I approach life's challenges. I often anticipate the worst possible scenario in every challenge. Then, instead of proactively addressing the challenge or participating I always stepped away and examined or reflected upon it.[9] I tended to find myself "outside" of the situation looking at myself. My father once told me that I was analyzing things too much and I

[9] It is commonly believed that the schizophrenic's inefficient processing of external reality eventually causes him to withdraw socially. (Bernheim Lewine, 1979)

guess he was right. I have also often thought of myself as worthless. Yet, at the same time, when I did feel some self - worth and validity, I would think that others secretly resented or were jealous of me. Sometimes I have even been suspicious that others wanted to hurt me, when there usually wasn't actually anything "wrong" happening at all. Truthfully, I have experienced the worst case of paranoia[10] at times about how I thought others are perceiving me and one of my earliest instances of overwhelming paranoia happened in high school. So many experiences in my adolescent years really took a toll, but this one stands out, even years later.

At fifteen, when I began getting really interested in boys, Shelley, by this time more of an acquaintance than an actual friend, brought me along with her on a double date, since we still got together occasionally. I had no idea who I was set up to be with and the whole thing was a complete surprise. When they arrived, my date was the driver and Shelley was in the back seat with her date. As we drove around, looking for a party, I began to feel very threatened – actually, the correct term is paranoid. The tension in the air was so 'thick' as I felt Shelly's watchful eyes on me in the back seat ... *then, I began to hear voices for the first time during this isolated incident, although I couldn't totally define "my voices", then, and wasn't fully aware of "them" until after I graduated from high school. My voices kept distracting me and intruding as I sat there motionless. They commented about me, persecuted me and frighteningly sounded a lot like demons ...*

My date also seemed agitated for some reason, and I was wondering, "Is this guy driver a terrible guy?" "Is that why?" "Is he fine, but he just doesn't like me?" "Is there something wrong with me?" Yet, that evening, as always, I still managed to play the attractive fun loving girl, who always smiled and who was

---

[10] A mental disorder characterized by delusions as of grandeur or especially, of persecution (WEB MD).

always nice, despite the subtle manipulations and rude distractions. The truth was that it was the most painstaking, embarrassing situation that I had ever been in. While we were together, all of us in the car, I questioned the validity of how nice I really was. Was I really being selfish and only worried about myself? Is that why I was so quiet? Did I actually deserve this? I wanted to talk to everyone so badly but was so afraid of failing! Then as we drove around looking for the party it all seemed even more strange because we couldn't find it. A song by Van Halen, a popular music group at the time, came on and I was literally becoming unglued. I can't stand that "mean-spirited" song even today and wondered at that time if Shelley actually intended to be mean. After that car incident, I realized that I somehow had to accept the reality that Shelley was no longer my perfect friend and I would never feel right around her at all. For a time, I continued to feel, deep inside, that she was still very nice and that the problem was actually with me but then, later I would suspect that Shelley had set up a disappointing date intentionally - *Shelley, who I looked to like a favorite icon*!

One of the last times we ever spoke with each other, Shelley - the only girl I ever trusted, admitted that she had guilt for what she had done to me. I didn't know what to say at the moment she told me that. I had always been used to her having it all together. It was a very fragile friendship between us and I finally realize that now - and, yet again, "The FACE" was the secret reason.

In Hiding (2007)

When you don't know that you have

33

something medically or psychologically
wrong it can be even more devastating
just trying to cope with a mystery (p.53)

Enchantment (2008)

Love

Love is a random
occurance
for those lucky
enough to find it
After you climb
as high as you can
and you reach
'El Capitan'
Remember love
Love is waiting
to be found
Love keeps us
from surrendering

CHAPTER THREE

Love and Mysteries

I believe that my father motivated me and gave me the tools necessary to sustain a level of achievement growing up before I was diagnosed with schizophrenia. His love and support despite his alcoholism, gave me courage, a foundation to stand upon, and he also taught me art. Because of his encouragement when I was young, males were a friendly distraction, but they were also where I attempted to find the degree of devotion and support I received from my often absent father. By the time I turned 14, I had also reached a certain awareness: the realization that my parents weren't perfect. I became critical of them, as teenagers often do. Then, I made a great male friend and confidante who was a fireman, artist and friend of the family. He was also a very talented painter, himself, creating beautiful ocean landscapes during his time off.

All of the neighborhood kids came to the fireman's door, but most important, he was a safe reliable friend for me to talk to. He had ideas a mile long, some of which were a little "quirky" or boring to listen to, but he did provide me with one important insight. When I told him about my social anxieties, he reassured me that "It's not always important to talk, but that just being with someone is what's important." This insight had a profound impact on me and I still carry that with me today. He remained a friend of the family for a long time even rescuing my family from homelessness later on in my life.

When I turned 15 I would also meet another male with whom I had my first romantic experience. I will call him "Irish" because he was almost full blooded Irish. Irish was a little rough around the edges with an appropriate "Irish temper", but on the other hand, appropriately the most cheerful person I had ever met. I felt comfortable around him, but once again, not as comfortable with other people, as I would soon come to find out when we were both working at the Summer Youth Employment Program. One day, we headed together for the Los Angeles County Zoo along with a busload of children we were supervising for the outing. We were both getting paid for this too, since the program was created so teenagers like us could transition easily into getting paying jobs on our own. I had a five year old boy to supervise for the trip and was singing an upbeat religious song with lyrics about Jesus Christ. I sung them surprisingly well (I thought so) as "Irish" looked on. It was a somewhat awkward song for me to sing, though, because my father didn't believe in Jesus Christ or in mainstream religion. He always preached about his Scientology "religious" beliefs instead.

Irish had a very prominent family and he was very intelligent so we talked like intellectuals together. I felt a "savoir-faire" with him and he seemed very interested in me. Confident that I would be ready for it, I agreed to go with Irish and his family on a weekend trip to the beach. For the most part, the short vacation took my breath away. The two of us enjoyed the ocean view and climbed down the rocks so we could get to the sand. We also took a ride in his "Jeep". Then, before leaving Irish's father wanted to take a picture of us together and, suddenly, I felt uncomfortable around his dad and the positive feelings about the vacation ended with a very "creepy" feeling. In an instant, I had what could be described as a "sinking", "twisting", "narrow escape" from "The FACE" as the camera snapped our picture! I had thought that horrible feeling was all behind me! I was afraid of showing my embarrassment, even though (as it turned out) the picture did not look that weird after all. I remained "shaken up" from that fateful event, trying hard to accept what had happened in my mind, but I couldn't. Even after guitar lessons, trips to the movies and a romantic trip to the mountains together, I still felt shaken up from that day on!

Then, at the beginning of my sophomore year in high school,

36

my family moved away from Irish, Shelley, and the city of Pasadena. I was sixteen when we moved and it wasn't easy adjusting to our new military beach city, Port Hueneme, a sleepy little town in Ventura County. My mind seemed mysteriously quiet during my first glances at what I saw around me. It had unbearably smaller buildings and fewer trees than those I had become accustomed to when living in Pasadena. It also was even harder for me to adjust to my new high school compared to the higher-paced school social life in Pasadena. I noticed right away that it was very strange for me to be in Port Hueneme now, especially after my previous and very difficult adjustment to Pasadena. In Port Hueneme there was also very few blacks, which made my interracial family seem even more different. All of a sudden, I felt as if I was different and too high strung compared to the other people that lived there in my new town. I still did my best to 'fit in', though, and tell myself that it was "a new beginning", but I missed Irish right away.

The course of pain and unbearable anxiety that I was now experiencing in Port Hueneme, my new school, and the prospect of making new friends, put me under a lot of pressure. I needed an anchor like Irish - and painfully so, but it had not worked out that way. I would have stayed indefinitely with Irish or even married him in my search for normalcy, but I soon realized that I had to break off our relationship because of my inner turmoil in Port Hueneme. Later in life, I hated what I had done and tore off "my half" of our picture together leaving only Irish's memory. As time went on, tearing my face from pictures would later become a bad habit for me.

I thought that Hueneme High was a small, flat, unattractive school but eventually, in a sense, it would seem to welcome me. I harnessed an unexpected sense of courage in all of my classes, but my art class was the most memorable for many reasons. For one, I met a "fellow artist" there who became somewhat of a soul mate and a faithful friend for most of my time in high school. He was a "Sweetheart," my teenage crush, and he even would become an obsession for me, so I will affectionately call him "Sweetheart." He made all of the awkward "boyfriend first advances" and we went to the Ventura County Fair for our first date. I didn't know whether to be thrilled, calm, content, or something totally different, and I was later surprised to discover the mutual devotion we would share. However, the pain of this mysterious schizophrenic disease I have, again, began to gnaw away at me and I had to continually remind myself of how handsome he was and of how very lucky I was to have him.

Then, one day, it was getting close to Thanksgiving and "Sweetheart" wanted us to experiment with marijuana. It seemed we both had some anxieties about it at first, but after reluctantly smoking it, I didn't notice anything right away. I just wanted to "go out" somewhere so we decided to go to an evening high school football game. We often rode our bicycles together, so we arrived at the game on our bikes, and it was early evening, just after dark. The entire experience soon became extremely uncomfortable for me ...

> ... *Even though it was just getting dark, it somehow seemed suspiciously dark. The atmosphere felt gigantic! I felt like, if I looked any harder ... I'd see the planets as well as everything else - all jumbled together! People seemed to be rushing past me ... I started to panic at the unbelievable energy around me. I felt assaulted by the street lamps ... the only light ...*

Immediately, I did not want to be at the football game anymore. The marijuana had produced a profound effect on me, but "Sweetheart" still appeared impressionable, despite it all, so we got on our bicycles and left after only a few minutes. I became very uncomfortable about marijuana from then on. Yet, without any drug or any interaction to speak of with anyone else, I always would begin to feel "off" sensations and perceptions like those I had experienced that night. I would feel that others were invading my space, stepping into the disheveled parts of my mind. Still unknown to me at the time, I now believe these intrusions were the result of my cognitive abnormalities and not the experience of marijuana. As a result, I grew less and less willing to go hardly any place. The only major exception was that every Sunday my new only friend, "Sweetheart" and I would go to the Swap Meet with his parents. While I was still in high school, my father eventually called me "boy crazy" on one of our visits and he couldn't have defined me better. I realize now that I was, in essence, attempting to replace *him*, the father who I hardly ever saw, with each new boyfriend. In my entire lifetime I think I only saw my father 35 to 40 times before his death, which isn't really much time at all. Yet, I still worshiped him and I now think that, deep down, he understood this. Later on he would also begin to feel strongly that I was wasting a lot of my own talent and opportunities by constantly seeking male attention.

I also learned a lot from my father's Scientology "lessons" which, looking back, were a near brainwashing experience. He loved to have a beer and tell me all that he believed. He also used Scientology principles in order to convince me that my mother was actually an "SP" or a "Suppressive Person".[11] According to Scientology, suppressive people should be avoided and guarded against because they are spiritually harmful to others. He also gave me a Scientology book on "How to Choose People". It explained that "man has to be right" and that "man is basically good".[12] All of these lessons and many more on the "positive side" may have actually helped me. During that time period, I was also extremely influenced by music and listened to just about every genre, even wishing I could enjoy more rock and roll music than I already did. Secretly, I began to wonder why some

---

[11] A suppressive person is a term used in Scientology for a person who seeks to suppress or squash any betterment, activity or group. (Hubbard, 2001)

[12] "The basic nature of man is not bad. It is good. But between him and that goodness are fears, rages and repressions." (Hubbard, L. Ron 1972)

types of music bothered me so badly. My own "sense of self" in regard to music and many other things was painfully absent.

I was also feeling a little frustrated most of the time at high school. After all, I felt I had to be enthusiastic with everyone there as a coping mechanism, most of the time - yet I was looking for comfort *everywhere*. I still wanted to be the "nice girl" everyone liked, kind of like Shelley, and for most of my teenage and early adult years, a series of similar "subconscious identity crises" would cause me to make a sequence of drastic decisions in my relationships with others. This "identity" problem is another trait of schizophrenia.[13] Studying and school work also remained difficult for me as I continued to have problems listening in class and reading. My concentration was also still very poor, especially when I attempted to watch documentaries in History and English class. I always panicked when I had to write about a documentary that I had seen because I would sit in front of a film, without the ability to pay any attention to it, pretending that I was watching, listening and participating. I always faked it by writing some comments about the film that came out of nowhere.

To this day, I don't know how I got through high school because I sometimes even got "D's or "F"s for grades. I just still kept on trying really hard to live up to my full potential. My parents both strongly believed in me and kept reminding me to stay achievement oriented. I didn't skip school very often, but I always had to make up for doing poorly at some things by working harder at others. For instance, I would work hard to create an excellent book report or study really hard for a test. Art Class and some other subjects also worked out well for me. I naturally excelled in art, especially in my drawings and pastel portraits of successful, famous people, so I entered my artwork

---

[13] "A firm sense of one's own autonomous identity is required in order that one may be related to in one human being to another ... otherwise any and every relationship threatens the individual with loss of identity. (Torrey, 2001)

in competitions, hoping to win a college scholarship.

I still desperately wanted a girlfriend at my new high school or nearby in my neighborhood, but all of the girls I had conversations with scared me and made me anxious. I would initially engage with them, but then I would soon feel distracted, "panicky" and suspicious. I also concentrated on trying to be graceful during social interactions which was really difficult to do. I don't know why but I couldn't stand someone else talking to whoever I was having a conversation with, and when that happened, I always felt as if I was being turned around in space! It felt like a mysterious force was sometimes trying to overtake me.[14] However, again, I had no clue at the time, that something really serious was wrong with me. On one occasion, I was invited to a girl's house who seemed as if she wanted me for a friend. I was interested at first, only to soon suspect that I was suddenly being ignored by her. I found myself trying to interpret her actions and analyzing everything, instead of just comfortably participating with what was going on and communicating with her. She was showing me her room, then I felt more paranoid when, suddenly, she left the room and I immediately thought she was "fleeing" me. It felt, when this occurred, like a feeling of total failure and sudden dread.

Desperately, I still tried to act interested and involved, but when I followed her to the front room, she would not even look at me. So, I made an excuse and left. At the same time, I wondered if she knew what was going on inside my head. That day, I was disappointed, most of all, that she had been so inconsiderate of my feelings. Now, thinking back, I believe I just anticipated the worst due to the anxiety I was getting from my obsessive thoughts and behavior. Everything like that always seemed to happen to me in "flashes", but these were not too overwhelming yet, like they would become later on. All the

---

[14] "In the broader culture the schizophrenic is the victim of external forces (the organic illness) that afflict him and over which he has no control or responsibility for." (Robbins, 1993)

same, they were still very frustrating. I would learn much later on, in 2012, that this uncontrollable behavior and obsessive thinking is also associated with generalized anxiety disorder which is a condition of it's own. It could have been possible too, now that I look back, that this new possible friend may have had some anxieties of her own. I do know that the experience with her was totally degrading for me, despite what the social situation may have really been about. I also know, now, the painful truth that schizophrenics like myself typically demonstrate an inappropriate emotional response and loss of empathy for others.[15] Could it be that I was just tired? Could it have been that deep down I didn't want a female friend? At the same time, I had so much social anxiety that it *was impossible* for me to relate to her.

During that time period, I was also lacking the social skill of asserting myself. This, I would eventually find out was a skill that I desperately needed when I became the target of a hostile co-worker at my first job. I had already worked at McDonald's for over a year when I suddenly became the target of another girl who worked there. This girl, who also worked during my shift would always *purposely* invade my space. For example, she would get in the way when I was wiping a counter or she would storm after me while I went to the lobby to clean up. When she did that, she really humiliated me but I never took it personally - I just ignored her. I mistakenly had developed the idea, by that time, that asserting myself would be evil and that bullies were exceptionally evil. In denial, I always told myself I was going to be "special" and different and not affected by all of that. I figured it was *her own problem* and it never turned into violence between us or anything worse. I learned later in therapy that I was actually trying at the time, by not asserting myself, to run away from anger.

I felt my anger would really get found out if "The FACE"

---

[15] Empathy: an ability to share in another's emotions, thoughts or feelings. (Webster's New World Dictionary, 1990)

ever showed itself. Because of my illness, I was actually having a lot of trouble having the full array of emotions and expressing them like everyone else did.[16] I also felt that I really wasn't this beautiful looking nice girl that I was trying to convey to others. Yet, despite my problems - or *because of my hard work and constant effort*, I was still promoted to working the drive-thru window and I felt so proud of myself. The manager even asked me to become a Hostess for McDonald's in charge of children's birthday parties. I also read stories to kids at the library on weekends. I felt successful enough at McDonald's and was managing my life, for the time being, without ever asserting myself at all. Today, looking back, I still don't know how all that I did then was even possible without doing so. At this point in time, I was also still feeling lucky to have my understanding and compatible boyfriend "Sweetheart' after the prior incidents with my girlfriend and other girls. I thanked God every day for my relationship with him and we had a lot of fun together. We used to ride our bicycles, 25 miles from Port Hueneme to Lake Casitas and back in one day and we even went to Yosemite with his parents, as well as to San Francisco with my own family.

"Sweetheart" and I would both receive best artists in the high school yearbook which was also significant to me, although I wasn't so lucky to win the full art scholarship I had hoped for when I graduated. I *was* awarded an Art Grant of one hundred dollars from a major local art organization, I designed a float for my high school class and I also participated on the yearbook committee. Given my struggles in class, I was also really surprised to get the Academic Fitness Award when I graduated. Yet, despite all of these positive experiences in high school, my relationship with "Sweetheart" unfortunately began to take a turn for the worse during our Senior year. My obsessive thinking was causing me to panic more often and I was suddenly getting

---

16 People tend to think act and feel all in one piece. The schizophrenic struggles with this. (Bernheim, Lewine 1979)

depressed for no reason that I was aware of at the time. I began to feel that "Sweetheart" was just too good-looking and became threatened by his ability to make friends - and even his ability to just concentrate on things that I couldn't focus on. I had always obsessed about his good looks, the experience of living by the ocean, or any other thing I could think of, but now the manic highs of that were fizzling out. He suddenly seemed a mile away from me and my mind wandered a lot as we watched TV. I shouldn't have been so jealous and suspicious, but I couldn't help it. "Sweetheart" had come out of his shell and I hadn't.

I really didn't think much about my emerging mental problems at the time. It just seemed to me then like my relationship with Sweetheart was taking a terrible turn. I recognize now that my high school relationship with him was actually the beginning of my obsessive behavior (manifested by repeated thoughts)[17] which can coexist, in some cases, with schizophrenia. I did not learn about all of this until much later and my obsessive symptoms were not successfully treated until 2014, long after my schizophrenia diagnosis. Schizoaffective disorder (my 1993 diagnosis) was finally my ultimate diagnosis due to my schizophrenic symptoms, along with the added presence of bipolar illness concurrent with normal moods at times. These bipolar moods, in my own case, were often either very happy or very depressed. These over-powering facets of my illness were beginning to have a stronger power over me while I was still dating "Sweetheart" but he, like me and like others in my life, had no idea, whatsoever, about my illness at that time.

My life was actually beginning to fall apart. I had already held four jobs in Port Hueneme, by this time, which were not successful and, all of a sudden, whatever magic the city of Port Hueneme once held for me seemed dull and unimportant. "The

---

[17] Various symptoms of obsessive compulsive disorder (OCD) are sometimes associated with or can even co-exist with schizophrenia. (Newsweek Zabludovsky 2001)

FACE," a persistent nightmare was also relentlessly tearing away my resolve and it felt now like I was on the verge of exposing my secret conflict at every waking moment! Making matters even worse, Sweetheart had no interest in graduating anymore or in any career goals either and I took that seriously. When he didn't graduate, on top of everything else, it was just too much for me. I decided I HAD to break up with him. I also decided to pursue life with a renewed promise of starting over - I was going to make it on my own! I kept believing that, if I just had the right people around me, "The FACE" would never show up on me again. I also thought there was someone out there who would make me feel more normal - someone on the "right" level of the Scientology tone scale. According to what I had learned, "Sweetheart" and I were no longer emotionally right for each other, in my opinion at that time.

I never really knew much about the broader aspects of Scientology due to my father's absence throughout my life and, now, at the age of 48, I realize that even what I *did know* about Scientology then, could not have made me more wrong than I was! I now take the blame, myself, for being too quick to be philosophical, or critical, and distant from others. I was using the religion of Scientology for my own form of self-diagnosis and to diagnose other people, instead of getting a thorough psychiatric evaluation and the appropriate assistance. I was also keeping almost all my thoughts and fears to myself at the time. Yet, I still do believe today that, maybe, without access to some of Scientology's principles I could have been even worse off. What could have been, or would have been without what I learned from Scientology will always be a real mystery to me.

I was very determined to succeed in the world after I graduated and I thought that all of my problems would be over now that I was free of being thrown into the "mix" of high school life. I was newly confident, optimistic and in a big hurry to be independent and live on my own. So, my mother, still unaware of my many silent fears and serious secret symptoms, agreed to help pay the cost of a room for me to rent. It was a wonderful room close to the ocean with a sliding glass door to the beach - enchanting and dream-like. It almost made me feel like a real taste of a better life was within my reach. I felt now like I was someone who was very special. The older fireman I once built a friendly relationship with was still in touch with us, so he attended my graduation and even helped me buy a car. Things were surreal and I was getting a taste of a dream that was really a nightmare unfolding. My father had come to visit my room once, but unfortunately he and I were drifting farther and farther apart because of his alcoholism and because he said I reminded him of my mother. He had not bothered to attend my high school graduation and the conflict with him now was about the boys in my life and about my mother. In the end, the worst of his displeasure with me would emerge from the fact that I didn't use Scientology to the extent that he wanted me to. I had not become active in the Scientology Church and organizational life and later on I, too, would become the "villain" myself and be considered an "SP" (suppressive person) by him - just because I started seeing a psychiatrist.

At age 18, after leaving "Sweetheart", my first serious delusions would begin to appear but, for a short while, I still remained optimistic. After graduating, I soon obtained a full-time job at Denny's restaurant in Port Hueneme and was told by the manager that teamwork was very important among the employees. Apparently, all of the other girls thought so too, because they would sometimes even get my plates for me when I was delayed picking them up from the cook's window. The managers and waitresses there were all easy to get along with and everyone supported each other in this positive, productive environment. In a sense, I was in a whirlwind to have such a job and I even felt very ambitious sometimes. Working at Denny's was a great accomplishment for me and I felt proud of myself. Despite "The Face", my voices, and my other woes, I was truly excited at this point to have found a waitress job where everyone was respectful and nice toward me.

I was so happy at this job, but still, after getting off work, I would feel depressed, even living in my beautiful beach side room. A waitress at Denny's who was very nice had befriended me, so my new girlfriend and I went to the Navy bars nearby and had some fun together. With her I was able for a short time to get caught up in the happy feelings of having a female friend again, meeting new people and sometimes even going to parties. There were many late night trips together to Denny's for their Decadent Chocolate Cake. I also become involved, briefly, with two different Navy guys, then soon scolded myself for being promiscuous as my negative inner dialect became more and more overbearing. Schizophrenics have tremendous trouble with how they perceive things, but I didn't know this at that time. I still tried really hard to maintain a positive attitude but, more and more often, I began to have very little desire to socialize anymore or to even do art. My life was becoming socially exhausting, full of anxiety and uneasiness.

I still was trying so hard to work and "play act" my life and I now even resented others for caring more than I did about social situations. Watching others socialize caused me to begin to wonder what the point of it all really was. I was confused about socializing and it seemed that I could only feel comfortable "one on one" with another person. Being in the presence of only one companion at a time had always seemed to be enough for me and, as I lived alone now, and withdrew from other people more and more, I almost forgot what it felt like to be social. When I *was* in the presence of others, the voices that constantly commented were "taking the wheel," and leaving me exhausted, but I didn't know that my inner world was actually becoming such a distraction. I read later that as schizophrenia develops in someone, "an inner world of fantasy comes to replace the outer world of reality" (Bernheim Lewine 1979). When I was alone in my room I now felt very alienated and totally alone in the world. It was also confusing to me because although I did not want to socialize, at the same time, I was sad that things seemed hopeful sometimes at work but so empty in my room.

I also had developed persistent doubts about how much my new girlfriend from work really cared about me. It had begun to seem as if many times she would only call me to "hang out" when she needed a ride. Despite the fact that she really *did seem to want to show me a lot of fun*, I never could seem to appreciate it. Instead, because of my developing illness, I began to feel the worst possible - that my newest female friend did not respect me and was probably just using me. I quickly became paranoid about her too, and even with the customers at work. The other waitresses at Denny's continued to be nice to me, seeming to know I was conflicted and didn't take it any further. My blunted emotions would eventually turn into depression, though and, after only a few months, my job at Denny's began to cause problems for me. Ultimately I felt alienated from everyone because I desperately desired to be like the other waitresses - I also felt I was somehow missing out on "all the fun". Then, my recent Denny's girlfriend, with whom I had fondly shared Denny's Decadent Chocolate Cake and Navy bars, had a baby and moved to Missouri. Unfortunately, after only writing to each other a few times, we lost touch with each other.

Later, during that same year, the real trouble in my life would begin ...

CHAPTER FOUR

A Disease Silenced Me

A cook named Francisco at Denny's had kept teasing me, saying that I was a "witch", but he was so cheerful, playful and flirtatious about it, that I didn't feel totally debased by his words. Also, since my father's ideology about spiritual awareness was so profound I found Francisco's nickname for me, along with his personality to be quite interesting and captivating. Nevertheless, it still made me a little paranoid. After all, he didn't know me very well and that was a powerful statement. I dated him briefly but often would just spend my time off from work, alone in my room listening to music and torturing myself. It seemed as if the young men that I really wanted to date didn't seem interested in me anymore. I attribute this, now, to my poor self-esteem and depression during that time period. Shelley came to visit me at work one time, but it still seemed I couldn't get under or over her walls.

A more questionable frame of mind seemed to emerge in me, along with "voices", and I began to think that this was what was keeping me from creating art. I also felt the voices, although still somewhat elusive at times, were extremely frustrating and interfering with my life too. I believed now that the voices *actually wanted me to keep thinking of them* - instead of doing my art and for the first time I wondered what was *really* going on. I confided in my mother, at the time, that I felt the "spirits" (which were actually my inner voices) were dangerously intruding and were now becoming a hindrance for me. She gently affirmed and reassured me that there were only "good spirits" and suggested that I talk to a therapist about my problems. She believed strongly in therapeutic help and, given her experience with her own mother's paranoid schizophrenia, she was really beginning to get a little uneasy about some of the

49

things I was saying.

I remained convinced that I didn't need psychiatric help and, instead, started searching for any other answer. I read a religious self-help book by Norman Vincent Peale called "The Power of Positive Thinking"[18] and prayed while I hung out in the lobby of Denny's on my days off. I also continued to miss my father at lot and I was in heaven during the few times I visited with him. However, my father *could get really angry*, at times, and often – unexpectedly! One time he had come to visit me and we were driving around together near the naval base in Port Hueneme. I began sharing some of the insights I was gaining from Norman Vincent Peale who I explained to him was actually a minister. Then – seemingly, from out of nowhere he got really red-faced and raised his voice really loud and said "Goddammit! There is no Jesus Christ!" I thought at that moment that my father was going to shove me or do something else to me – and for reasons that were unrelated to religion! It was really weird and intimidating.

The resident-owners of the beach house, where I was still renting a room were extremely quiet and nice, but they had a rebellious 10 yr. old daughter and a very bashful 6 yr. old son. They were a husband and wife sales team for Amway and I often wondered what really went on behind their smiles. They eventually lost the wonderful house on the beach, after only four months of renting me my room, but I moved with them to a different house on the other side of town. That house was just as nice as the other house was and they gave me the largest bedroom with an adjoining bathroom. The couple expressed a genuine interest in me when they once asked me to play "The Greatest Love of All," a song by Whitney Houston for their daughter. It touched me deeply that they showed an interest in sharing such an experience with me.

I loved the new room just as much but I felt so lonely living

---

[18] "The Power of Positive Thinking" (1992) by Norman Vincent Peale is a religion based book with powerful, inspirational messages and lessons about faith.

there. I often took a drive in my car and continued to hang out at Denny's on my time off. However, despite their reassurance and the wonderful accommodations, I was feeling as if something else was wrong after a few more months at that point. I was also beginning to hear more voices. I felt so "infected" by what I thought were "spirits in my head" (voices) that I thought maybe my Amway landlord roommates could actually hear those persistent inner voices which often cruelly commented about them. These delusions were only the beginning of what was to come. When they decided to move yet AGAIN, I thought it was really my fault that, suddenly, I didn't have a room to rent anymore.

My own family was now living in Old Town Ventura a beach town just a few miles from Port Hueneme. Now, with no place to live and in a new, unfamiliar frame of mind – still hearing those voices, off and on, constantly - I decided to move back in with my mother. By this time, Ventura, even with it's enchanting allure, did not bring much relief from all of my continuing anxiety. I started to become really worried about my future, but I was only 19 years old and still did not realize, at that time, the real magnitude of my illness. I suffered a growing sense of frenzy about social situations which by now resulted in a total disinterest and avoidance of them. I'd go to the artsy, quaint coffee shop called Franky's just down the street from where we lived and just stare into space - trying to find an identity - or at least to imagine I was someone normal - trying to find someone I would like to act like. Instead, my focus remained on others evaluation of me, so I quickly lost the interest in being at the coffee shop.

Now, stuck alone in my room on my days off, afraid to do anything because of the voices, I tried to cope. I had a friendly little pet love bird that kept me company in my room, but my pet "Judy Bird" often got very noisy much to everyone else's irritation. Always introspective and philosophical, I tried hard to analyze why the voices were continually there. I began to feel that they were perhaps being implanted in me and that I couldn't help but focus on them. Since the breakup with "Sweetheart" had been very painful, I was also now having trouble concentrating on anything but him, so I began to get angry, suspecting that *he* was implanting an evil spell in me! He would not leave my thoughts!

Then another new terrifying symptom emerged. I began to think I was telepathic. I had been reading another book, this time by Ray Bradbury, one of my father's favorite science fiction/fantasy authors. I now believed that I could communicate with others by just using my thoughts. (I didn't know it at the time, but this is also a frequent belief expressed by people who suffer from schizophrenia, schizoaffective, and other mental disorders.[19])

I began trying to rid myself of the pain by "broadcasting" thoughts which I believed "Sweetheart" was receiving[20] and then I would feel really guilty sometimes afterward. Then, sometimes I thought "Sweetheart" was hearing my unloving thoughts and getting hurt, so I would become extremely ashamed. I would also sometimes feel that, by doing this, I was just clearing my mind. I did meet with "Sweetheart" once during this time and surprisingly, he was doing well. He loaned me a 'Simply Red' music cassette and I really didn't see him much after that.

Moving to Ventura had been another new beginning for me and I reminded myself that this was exciting and good for me at times. My mother had a shop on Main Street selling lingerie and I made a beautiful sign for her store with a logo that I had designed myself. I also designed logos for two other business

---

[19] Sudden, unintentional intrusive thoughts are a prime symptom of schizophrenia. These are often accompanied by the delusional belief that the thoughts are being inserted by others into one's mind ("thought insertion"). For the schizophrenic, it is as if a neurological gating process has failed to inhibit internal stimuli. (Snyder 1993)

[20] Thought broadcasting is the belief that one's thoughts are being broadcasted from one's head and can influence the external world. (Miller, Keane, 2003)

men who were friends of my mother's at the time. I was ambitious and very eager to stay even more occupied, which I expressed to my mother, so she tried patiently and hard to build my confidence. She reminded me that I was just sensitive and that things would always work out. I would buy dresses from the money I earned at Denny's and my mother would tell me which ones she thought looked best on me. At the same time, she was also beginning to suspect that something was seriously wrong with me, but I think she also knew I was wrestling" with the conflict I was experiencing between seeking therapy, which she had suggested that I do - or to follow my father's wishes and find a solution through Scientology.

Suddenly, however, without the ability to draw from many recent or pleasurable experiences with my father, he was now beginning to become a painful memory for me. We hardly ever saw each other. He had always tried to help me, mostly through writing letters, but my father didn't *really* know about all of the symptoms I was experiencing. When I would share my problems and fears with him, he would always assure me in his letters that he had ways of "handling it" with Scientology. When "handling it" never happened, I began to think he might be kind of "nutty" and just an imaginative alcoholic in a different universe. He would always say to me, "Okay, now I am "auditing" you (this is a Scientology term for acting as a listener/ facilitator) and I appreciated his efforts, but it wasn't fully working for me. Despite my respect for him, I did not desire seeing him as much anymore.

In his absence, I continued to look for more answers to explain why I was thinking "differently". I began to feel that maybe I was just living in the wrong place and started to dream of a faster paced lifestyle like the one I had experienced in Pasadena. Then, still in denial - and still avoiding therapy - I began my own self-analysis, based on my father's ideas about mass media. He had always stated that most sitcoms and music were poorly done, so I started to think that maybe my emotions were dulled because I was a real artist, but living in surroundings that were not stimulating enough for me. I decided that I was just bored with life, experiencing dulled emotions when I was not doing art. Later, after seeking professional help and getting diagnosed accurately, I found out that "it" definitely was not just that.

In fact, during times of extreme illness, throughout all of my life, I have always had dulled emotions towards the things that other people value. For instance, I often could not appreciate the smell of a flower or pay attention to the weather outside. I also found it painful or was sometimes even offended that others enjoyed such normal pleasant things. These dulled emotions applied to many, many other areas and things in my life and, perhaps, ultimately made me less appealing to others as an individual. I was unaware that my illness was always filtering through, even on those levels. I was also having mini-blackouts at the time. These are sudden very brief losses of one's cognitive functions. I also experienced voices, sometimes, that I was not always *fully* aware of - and from those grew a sense of even lower self-esteem and negativity. I was experiencing difficulties and fears that "auditing" would not be able to fix.

Despite my parents' positivity, encouragement, and efforts to help, I was also having another complicated problem. I often went to emotional extremes. If I was happy, I was really happy. If I was sad, I was really sad. If afraid, I was really afraid. Angry? Then, I was really angry. This tendency, I would eventually find out, was due to my schizoaffective disorder: manic-type, which was finally diagnosed much later in 1993. I always turned my anger inward which, as I also found later in therapy, caused extreme depression in my case.[21] I would end up hurting so bad because of the anger I held inside and suspected more, as time went on, that people just couldn't relate to me. All of my attempts at social interaction have been extremely difficult, for

---

[21] Internalizing anger can have harmful effects. It is debilitating, mentally and physically, causing cynicism and/or feelings of depression and victimization. (Josey, Bass 2014)

as long as I can remember, because of my "inner world".

It felt as if it was always weighing me down, or sometimes suffocating me, when just trying to ignore it, in social situations. Often times I would find myself wanting to get angry at inappropriate times, or silently wanting to cry out for no reason due to the pressure this inner world was causing. I was, unknowingly, full of rage inside, but on another level, I was also terrified. I would wake up in my sleep seeing spiders, as my suffering grew even more intense. Without the proper diagnosis and treatment for my illness, everything started to become more and more difficult to do and my life was gradually falling apart.

I tried so many different ways of coping, but no solution was ever permanent. Between the ages of 19 and 26 I would still continue to keep struggling with my faulty perceptions, still trying to keep jobs. I was always perceiving one outcome after another through my own misleading viewpoint. This is because, my conclusions were made from a schizophrenic's jurisdiction instead of from the "well" side of me. I tried very hard to escape my frame of mind but couldn't, even though the functioning side of me often, deep down, knew better. Finally, my "inner-world related nature" would come full circle and full-blown later on. *This is what happens to people with my illness until they get help and treatment.*

I started a new job at Bob's Big Boy that was closer to my home. It was successful for ten months, just like my first waitressing job at Denny's had been, but my stress level eventually took it's toll on me there too. Total paranoia began to settle into my illness, along with even more frequent delusions - and all of this began to affect me more and more. The manager at Bob's Big Boy who I will call Sara (not her real name) was very easy going and nice and liked "pal-ing" around with the waitresses which I was very nervous about. I felt she would dislike me for not being the "same" as the others and as sociable. It was difficult because I *did like* the other waitresses and felt, deep down, that I would *love* to be sociable with them. They were always helpful, like they had been at Denny's, with picking up a plate for me if I didn't pick them up on time, but I just still kept feeling overwhelmed around Sara, the boss. It was slowly becoming very obvious to me that I had always felt very uncomfortable, for some reason - and even a little terrified around other women – and especially uneasy working at a place where the boss was a female.

One day, at work, I accidently looked over my shoulder at Sara when she passed me. I thought she had noticed my paranoia because she looked right back at me too. Instantly, I now perceived a new problem with my boss, Sara. The "problem" was in my own mind - whether it was real with her or not. I believed she was going to begin to doubt my abilities. Then, she came up to me on my break and casually struck up a conversation, seemingly to find out what was going on. I just looked down panic-stricken, very ashamed, afraid, and avoiding eye contact with her. I felt like she had "found out" how conflicted about her I really was inside. I looked at her pleadingly and she initially responded with what I believe was a look of being interested in me. Yet, on the other hand, I also sensed she had a kind of 'bored' look about the situation.

It was now my opportunity to talk to her and explain everything, *so I really tried to* - but I kept looking down because of "The FACE." I finally looked up briefly and gave Sara my best "look of confidence". Then I got up, suddenly - and left the table. I had the feeling that I had ultimately lost control and given Sara the "brush off". *The 'brush off' was a smug look I would give, unintentionally, to someone when I was under pressure. It would usually be followed by completely ignoring someone.* By doing that, I could at least, feel some semblance of social control when I was so anxious. After all, I couldn't tell her the real truth! This would happen a lot to me during many future social interactions to come. (Note: I've learned now after receiving professional help, how *not to* accidently portray that behavior, thankfully. My increased comfort and sense of control is also due to now being successfully medicated for my condition.)

After my "brush off" I arrived to work one day only to find

Sara, (such a nice lady, I had always thought before) sitting at the corner of the cook's station staring at me looking kind of angry (I thought). She had decided to cut my work hours! I got up and walked out of the restaurant. This was the first of three consecutive waitress jobs where I now would just walk out of the workplace suddenly.

I realize now that my perceiving our interaction the way I had initially, was what ultimately caused the much bigger problem. (I would learn much, much more about my "perceptions" when I finally began therapy later on in my life) I also realize now that my dad's preaching had perhaps given me a false sense of security about my condition. I was actually in the grasp of a serious mental illness – one of the most mysterious and least understood illnesses in the world – schizophrenia. As I would soon find out - in my own case - I actually suffer from a somewhat less potent, but extremely disabling form of the illness, schizoaffective disorder, which is diagnosed when delusions are quite marked over a period of time and according to experts, is hard to diagnose.

This was the time in my life when I should have definitely gotten professional treatment, but I still believed that I would, somehow "handle it" as my Dad always said I would with Scientology. I always felt that somehow, someway there was something more I could learn from the religion of Scientology or from my own reading and research that would save me.

Our family actually lived up the hill from busy Main Street in Ventura. One day, after getting some coffee and feeling hopeful and cheerful, I was walking up the hill to get home and a seemingly strange kind of guy was staring at me from the furniture warehouse down the street. I decided not to be judgmental, thinking that maybe the love of a new boyfriend might provide a solution for me since I didn't have one single friend in my life anymore. He seemed "different" to me and "out of his element" somehow. He would always stand very stiff, staring from out of the back of the furniture warehouse where he worked every day, with what I can only describe as the look of a disturbed "Watchful Tiger" in his eyes. Initially, I felt a little frightened that maybe he might begin to stalk me, but I tried not to be too critical of his demeanor because I felt that could make his attitude toward me worse.

It would come as a pleasant surprise that this unusual and relatively 'short' "Tiger" showed up at my newest waitress job with a beautiful little white Teddy Bear for me! I appreciated his sweet gesture and how warm, welcomed and accepted it made me feel in the desperate, frantic corners of my existence. He was attractive to me and he did have muscles from working out. He also had a great job and seemed to have "something" going for him. I accepted his gift, began to think that maybe he couldn't really be all that bad after all, and forced myself to begin feeling more positive about him. My now new boyfriend who I will affectionately call "Red" would later move in with us for a brief time while we looked for our own apartment together. I felt okay about this arrangement for a while because my mother had discovered rats in the very charming old house we were renting and Red would chase them and try to kill them for us. He never got one, but we all thought it was hilarious.

I forgot my delusions for a while and began to enjoy my new relationship with Red. Now that he was my new boyfriend, the spider nightmares I was having also suddenly disappeared. Soon, Red and I moved in with his brother because my little sister, now a teenager, was having some problems of her own that I couldn't deal with. The three of us now shared a beautiful new three bedroom condo located in a great neighborhood. There was even a spare bedroom that we used for lifting weights and a beautiful swimming pool in the courtyard. I have always loved animals, and making things even better, his brother had two beautiful Cocker Spaniels. I spent my spare time reading Danielle Steele, my favorite romance author, in the courtyard by the pool. I even stopped broadcasting thoughts for a while and felt happy much of the time - at first.

Then, before too long, my still undiagnosed disorder began to haunt my new life more and more every day. I began to have a long succession of intrusive thoughts and then also started to imagine that Red had raped someone in the past and was now having sexual relations with the receptionist at his job. Since I believed that I really did have insight and could see into other's lives, my thoughts about Red really terrified me. In my past I had predicted other's behaviors very well and even had visions that came true, but I didn't understand why I was thinking these terrible things now. I realize now that these thoughts about Red were complete fantasies and total distractions.

Looking back, I may have been intentionally creating wild fantasies about Red to somehow distract me from the other intrusive thoughts that were constantly trying to flood in. I felt more in control when I thought of "my own" thoughts, instead of sudden unanticipated intrusions. I began to feel disgusted, disturbed and ashamed and, during my time with Red and would also try self-medicating by experimenting with alcohol and marijuana a few times. I even tried cocaine once, hoping to feel better. Thankfully, however, I was never the type to seek out the 'experience' of taking drugs on a daily or regular basis. If I had done that, my problems may have become much worse. I realize now that the real problem with my relationship with Red lay in the fact that he was verbally abusing me on a regular basis. I was never sure whether he would hit me, if I ever stood up to him or defended myself verbally, and wondered sometimes if being with 'Red' might lead to something really horrific.

I eventually went to a Pink Floyd concert with Red and his friend, nicknamed "Wingo," shortly before New Year's Eve. I was a little excited, at first, because I have always loved music. I also liked the band and it was better than being alone, by myself, at the condo. At the concert, all I could think about was whether people were staring at me or not. I grappled with my composure, but after a while, it became unbearably uncomfortable for me. I couldn't wait for the concert to end! Suddenly half-way through, and from out of nowhere, tears began to literally pour down my face and I began to beg to myself for them to stop! I didn't really feel that sad, at all, and I couldn't believe this was happening to me! The tears came from out of nowhere as if something from outside of my body was planting them there! Then, suddenly - they stopped - as mysteriously as they had appeared and, luckily, neither Red nor "Wingo" seemed to notice.

Looking back, it now seems that my life, at that time, was very unstable. I had moved three times within only a little over a year, so I constantly felt unsettled and anxious. I was also still a little confused about my mother - as I was about everyone else - but we were still keeping in touch. Red was abusive but he didn't try to interfere with my creative life or my employment. I was trying so hard to be a waitress because I felt it was a better job than many others, but I would always get into trouble or rejected, over and over, because of that effort. I was beginning to get frightened because, before the experience with Sara, it had been very unlike me to walk out on jobs – but I now began suddenly walking out of my waitress jobs. Also, I believe now that it was unrealistic for me to keep pursuing waitress jobs since I was never good at them.

During that relatively short time, while living with Red, I had also managed to get hired for and then to lose seven more different jobs after leaving Bob's Big Boy. Then, while still living with my somewhat abusive boyfriend I would work at a little specialty shop in the mall that I really liked – only to get fired from that. *I was trying so, so hard to have a normal job and a normal life!*

I still continued to try and try. My dad had always enjoyed working at pizza places, so I decided to get a job working at "Express Pizza", a little Mom & Pop place. Surprisingly, I actually really had no significant problems at that pizza job, because it was slow paced and much easier than the faster paced coffee shop waitress jobs. I was also alone at the counter quite a bit of the time, which made the job less stressful for me. Consequently, though, the job may have been "too easy" and given me a false sense of security or confidence. I would work at my pizza job for only five months before quitting.

Mervyn's department store, another job opportunity which

I eagerly anticipated, hired me in November 1987. I wore all my favorite dresses to work there and surprisingly, I loved the smell of new clothing and colognes that lingered throughout the store. I managed to hold a position for a while in the boy's department stocking the shelves and working the cash register. I was just certain it would lead to a more permanent position, but that would be a big mistake. I got promoted to the jewelry department, only to get sent back to where I was when I started there. Soon afterward, my hours were cut to a mere eight hours a week, so I quit. I was feeling now that, perhaps, I should have kept the less stressful job at the pizza place after all.

During this time, although I often felt insecure, l would also feel, in a certain regard, and for an assortment of different reasons - that I was *above everybody else*. This is also a common belief shared by people, like myself, who have schizophrenia or schizoaffective disorder. I rarely got sick (physically), so I even felt I had "superior genes". I also believed that I had a positive effect on my environment and that I was frequently touched by "divine inspiration". I kept continuing to think that if I could just connect with the right social network, I would ultimately succeed. I felt on one hand that I was superhuman ... however, deep down, I also suspected that somehow, I was ... as they say "missing a fuse". I was still in denial about my illness.

Eventually, I managed to get a really nice job as a waitress at The Elephant Bar in Ventura. It was a classy restaurant with attractive waitresses, frequented by all of the local business men, so I was extremely proud to be working there! Everyone at the workplace was also really nice to me and I believed this may have been the case, because there were a lot of other pretty girls there. So, I actually fit in! All of the waitresses complimented me or smiled at me sometimes. Surprisingly, I also didn't feel as nervous around the manager, either, who was an extremely nice gay woman. I felt at this point that my search for the perfect job had finally come to fruition. During the brief time I worked there I heard no voices, didn't feel stupefied by others walking

61

by, and basically had no symptoms. I eventually got fired simply for coming in only five minutes late for the third time.

I still remained extremely hopeful about my life most of the time, but I was also naive. I believed that if I was just nice to people and found the right connections in life I would not fail. I didn't think it was important to assert myself around others and I still continued to live with Red and to struggle with more jobs. I got a job at "Sears" but I forgot to clock out on the time clock once and as a result got fired from there, too. Next, I tried working at a Denny's restaurant in Ventura, and it was at that job that I had a *really* major delusion. This began to convince me - and others close to me - that perhaps, my mental condition was very serious - perhaps even incapacitating ...

Aspirations (2005)

*"I ignored the nagging voice that something was
really wrong with me and I tirelessly forced myself
to stay optimistic ..."*   (p. 72)

CHAPTER FIVE

Fantasies and Nightmares

My first major delusion occurred during my second employment, this time at Denny's, Ventura, and I was immediately disappointed at what transpired from that. I know now that this particular delusion was stress induced because I was extremely uncomfortable at that job. On my first day working there I sensed a certain distance from everyone and a powerful feeling of paranoia. The unmistakable major delusion that followed, along with my strangest experience yet, at the workplace, was about my parents. It came to me as my father's "voice". Feeling overwhelmed and already doomed at that job, I thought that, *if* I just paid really *close attention* ... I could hear my father' s voice more clearly ... my father said to me ...

"Now, you see what I have planned for you - your mother and I!" Then he continued ... *"Every step you have taken ... up until this time was planned ..."*

I analyzed from what I had just heard him say that the two of them - my parents - were *actually* witches, planting all of my thoughts in my head - totally controlling me and *all* of the events in my life!" I now believed that all of the places I had been to – along with everything - *all that had ever happened to me* - even when I was far away from my parents, had occurred because of a grand scheme conjured up by my mother and father! My life's events had actually *all been planned by them in advance!*

Now that I realized this, I soon visited my mother, informing her that *I knew* and was certain of this fact. I told her this - in order to *let her know* that *I now knew what they were doing!* In response, she attempted to tell me that from what I was saying to her, she was strongly convinced, at this point, that I really needed a comprehensive psychiatric evaluation and counseling. She went on to explain to me that I could possibly be having the same problems as my maternal grandmother had experienced when she had what in those days was called a nervous breakdown. Although I was really scared and insecure at this point, I still didn't listen to her until several years later, but I now accept the fact that biological background does represent a stronger risk factor for schizophrenia than social factors do.[22] At that time, I continued to resist, stating that I was NOT going to get involved with therapists and psychiatrists. I feared I would just become a another statistic just like I had often heard happened to other "unfortunate" people. As a result of not seeking help right away, I lost my latest job at Denny's.

Today, I still don't know why I didn't get the proper help at that time for my own well-being. Instead of doing this, I denied what was happening and praised myself that at least Denny's had experienced the initial desire to hire me. I also kept using positive "self-talk"[23] to convince myself that maybe working at Denny's was just not the right job atmosphere for me yet. I also made a major decision about another possible solution: to follow my father's advice and seek assistance from the local Church of Scientology. Desperate for help, despite my denial, I soon had signed up for a course there. I also invited Red to come with me and take the course too. Just being there, right from the beginning, would make me begin to think even more often about things like the nagging voices that were often in my head.

A question on the initial Scientology questionnaire asked us, "Do you believe your thoughts are your own?" I answered "Yes", but I had to carefully think about it. A nagging voice had always told me that my thoughts could actually be heard by others. My denial of the actual problems I had still remained very strong. I reminded myself that, after all, lots of people believe in "spiritual" things, like other "forces" or "voices" that guide them,

---

[22] Torrey, Fuller (2001)

[23] A method of internal self- preservation and affirmation (Saunders, 2005)

thereby reassuring myself that my own thinking was not that unusual or bad. I would continue, for the most part, to feel somewhat competent throughout my lessons at the Church of Scientology, except for one disturbing experience ...

One time, while Red and I were still taking the course, I began to think that our situation in that setting was somehow comical to me and I unexpectedly laughed in class. Then, I began to laugh some more and couldn't stop my laughter on cue. This quickly became painful and embarrassing for me because I temporarily felt that I had lost control of myself by laughing like that. The Scientology instructor seemed to understand, though, and didn't get upset about it. However, this still caused me anxiety, great pain and a feeling of failure. I now had come to realize that, even in this Scientology classroom setting, I couldn't stop my behavior or my emotions on cue.

I know now that my behavior in that class was actually another trademark of schizophrenia, but I didn't know it then. My uncontrollable laughter was due to the frequently noted inability of a person suffering from schizophrenia to control his or her emotions on cue. During moments like that, a schizophrenic person seems to be flooded by information, thoughts and feelings from within, along with stimulation from without. In other words he or she seems to have a faulty "shut off" mechanism or a "faulty filter" and as a result the mind gets overwhelmed.[24] This inability to sort out and discard emotions is still a very real - and potentially overpowering - hindrance for me and for people like me even today.

I continued my lessons at the Church of Scientology organization, but I eventually begin to feel less interested about improving my mental state of mind. I had primarily, all along, just been very curious about what the classes would offer and they were quite costly. I decided that I didn't really want to take the course any further than I had at the time. In contrast to me, Red, who had remained right by my side during the classes,

---

[24] Bernheim, Lewine 1979

really enjoyed the experience, so to speak, seemingly more than I did and probably got more out of it. Since I didn't really feel as many symptoms while spending time with Red, just the two of us together, I now felt that he was more worthwhile than the class for me. I also thought that I needed him for my everyday survival so he was more important to me. As a result I quit the class, even though I did enjoy taking that course most of the time and it was taught by a helpful and nice man. It was also kind of special having a boyfriend *with me* there who I thought really worshiped me.

I began attending Ventura College, still searching for my niche in life or career path as many young adults do in their early twenties. I wanted a way to contribute my talents to the world or even to just earn a living. It had a beautiful campus and seemed like it would serve as another possible solution for me. Going to college was also a helpful distraction from my problems, for a while, and I would continue taking classes there for two semesters. My most memorable experiences at the college would be the beautiful paintings I created in my Acrylic Painting class which I took for two semesters with a great teacher. He was a very intense man, friendly enough, but obviously absorbed by his own ego. He was the only art teacher I knew who would paint his own paintings during class and also boldly "touch up" his students' paintings -including one of mine. Art has always been a real lifeline for me, so my art classes in college had a powerful, but temporary, positive effect on my low self-esteem.

I was very proud of the paintings I did in college and I wanted them to be very unusual. People who walked by would even stop and stare at my work during class. I felt very confident as a painter, at that time, but unsure of exactly where my paintings would actually fit in. I asked my mother if I should take some paintings to a gallery and, attempting to be protective, she cautioned me that it can often be a "political thing" with some galleries. In other words, it wasn't always talent that motivated an owner to arrange a show for an artist. I

66

tended to agree with her about venturing into a fine art "gallery experience" for the time being. That seemed way too complicated for me. I now feel that my greatest paintings up until 1988 were created in that college acrylic painting class and I have saved them through many moves and transitions. "Sandbox", "Listening" (Madonna) and "Friendly Owl" were only a few.[25]

Feeling more confident about my future as an artist after this experience, I decided to also take a Commercial Art class at Ventura College. I hoped now to learn more about making art my new career goal as a profession. Unfortunately, the middle aged, very extroverted and talkative female teacher in that class always avoided eye contact with me. She virtually ignored me as I kept waiting for my turn to interact with and get feedback from her. I became really uncomfortable and would just stare at her and keep waiting. I felt as if she would never come my way to help me and then I ultimately began to fear that I was going to lose control of myself before that even happened. She would tend to look my way assertively which I always perceived as "angrily". It would be the first time in my life in an actual art class that I felt really inferior. Most likely because of this negative feeling, I would receive a "D" from her as a final grade.

I had never experienced that kind of resistance from a teacher and it really changed me. I had let her bad grade begin to define me, not only as an artist, but as a person. This was a turning point for me as a young woman. I had failed in what had always been a "comfort zone" for me. I also thought that with all of my abilities in painting, design and illustration, my grade was unfair and then blamed it all on "that awful teacher" from my commercial art class. I even began to suspect that maybe she had heard good things about me from my acrylic painting teacher or from other students in his class and resented me.

Today, the only thing I can remember gaining from that

---

[25] Several of my original paintings and illustrations are featured throughout this book. Also please see Appendix

class, was a bit of advice the "distant teacher" offered us one day. She looked *right* at me, as if speaking *only* to me, and advised the class, "never to use complementary colors in paintings because they are so dull." I had often used really bright complementary colors for my paintings, so I initially disagreed with her statement but, over time, I have learned to better downplay my use of complementary colors, though I still continue to use them. I now think that maybe, perhaps, something useful did come of what I had perceived as my teacher's terrible attitude, although during the following semester, I began to think that other students were looking at me strangely after that incident.

During my second semester at Ventura College, school became even harder and more socially challenging than high school had ever been. On the other hand, my Spanish class was a little different. I was always good at languages and I even developed a crush on my Spanish teacher. He told captivating stories and recited beautiful Spanish poems in class. He even threw a party at his home for the whole class, after which I eventually ended up feeling paranoid, too, because of the other girls that were there. I still managed to receive a B in his class because of my natural talent with Spanish. In contrast, I had extremely uncomfortable experiences in Jazz Dancing (which I initially thought would be very fun) and in my Anthropology class. Both of these classes were taught by women and I had trouble with both. I finally had to drop Anthropology and Jazz Dance with 'Fs' in both!

Ventura College was, by this time, turning out to be very disappointing. I was still in denial about my "developing" illness and, adding to my insecurities, I was always constantly surrounded, even sometimes enveloped by the dulled emotions and "faulty switch" I described earlier. Yet, despite all of this, I continued to hold on to my dreams about making a living with my art. My mother continued to encourage me and praise my art, while my father also built my confidence, at the time, even telling me I was a "born" illustrator. Because of their never ending encouragement, I continued to think that somehow, in some way, I could do it and make a living with my art, if only I had the right connections. I just had to figure out exactly how to do so and, hopefully, how to contribute to the world using the talent that, deep down, I always knew I had.

I also began to consider that maybe I really needed to go to an actual art school and to do whatever else was necessary to get work as a professional artist. I started to hope that someday maybe I would be able to further my studies at that level, even though most professional art schools were far away and very expensive. A counselor at Ventura College I spoke to about going to an actual art school seemed to be as uncomfortable as I was while we were talking and that also discouraged me. Overall, that experience with the counselor further complicated my problems with self-esteem. I finally concluded that making it in art would be too hard since I wasn't an extrovert and that it would take more money than I had available to me. I soon began to feel more detached and afraid to ask anyone else about it, yet, in the wake of all these experiences, I did feel as if I was just throwing away my art talent.

All of this was very painful for me and it wasn't long before I began to feel that my positive experiences with art in college had been "pointless". Therefore, even doing art, at all, was beginning to feel that way as well. Life itself was now seeming too powerful for me and I wondered what was really missing. Why did my teacher treat me like that? I judged her and myself, over and over again, and it started to make me angry. I had *tried so hard* in her class and in everything I attempted to do in life and *it all still was never enough*. Why couldn't I function? Why was nothing working for me? I still didn't know, at that time, that I had schizophrenia and I also thought, like most people do, that schizophrenia was a disease where you had a "split personality" or several multiple personalities.[26] I didn't

---

[26] Multiple personality or dissociative identity disorder is a different illness; patients are described as having at least two identities or dissociated personality states (Web MD 2015)

know I had anything at all.

When people asserted themselves toward me I always thought they were just being mean. Then I would curse myself for not being able to understand *how a person is supposed* to assert themselves so I could learn to do that myself. I was also confused about *whether* I was even supposed to assert myself and in what kind of situations was doing so actually necessary.

I would also ask myself *why* other people were sometimes so assertive and confrontational toward me? I would always wonder this because I *typically went out of my way to be friendly toward everyone*. I really thought I gave them no reason to be that way and I had built a mountain of emotional wounds inside because of the rejection I perceived from their assertiveness at that time. Ultimately, I felt that other students on campus and faculty members should be more understanding of me like it seemed some people had occasionally been during the more positive times in my life. Now, after only two semesters in college, it appeared that my experiences there were becoming less and less promising.

My refusal to get help, was also causing me to have more and more troubling thoughts. As time went on, it ultimately led to me blaming *myself as a person*. I thought that maybe I just wasn't a "good" human being. After all, I was the one who had grimaced and lost control, both of myself and of social situations so many times. "The FACE" I described earlier was still perpetually waiting – waiting to come out. Was this happening to me because I was being unnecessarily hateful? Who had said I was nice? Or maybe I still really, deep down, *just didn't care*? I asked myself these questions over and over. Beating myself up in this manner would keep happening for me up until my thirties.

Meanwhile, I was now almost 21 years of age, still living at the beautiful condo with Red, and thinking I was happy. I didn't really need to work, during that time, and probably should have felt even more fortunate than I actually felt about my situation. I was even reading romance books instead of internal broadcasting, then, which was a positive experience for me. Sometimes I would feel sad, though, even at times when there wasn't any actual thought to correspond with that despondent feeling.[27] Something serious was going on inside me now, as if I was being "swept away", but still only by a gentle breeze. I couldn't really figure it all out, but I did know I was constantly feeling overwhelmed by unexpected emotions at inappropriate times. It even happened to me when I was alone or while doing otherwise "healthy" activities.

It also scared me that one of those powerful emotions was a sudden unexpected fear or paranoia sometimes, even without any specific thought to back that feeling up. I wanted to feel better, to feel "normal", but my father continued to tell me that I just needed to get audited, which was the Church of Scientology's replacement for psychiatric treatment or talk therapy.[28]

Sadness and hurt now felt in some way familiar and comfortable to me and, in 1988, after living in the condo with Red for almost two years, Red's brother eventually heard me crying one day in the bedroom. I was sad about my family detachment, my art, and about any other excuse that I could think of to feel sad. He felt uneasy about this and told Red he was going to move out of the condo we all shared and live with his new fiancé. Since Red and I had been renting our room from his brother and I had no job at the time to help pay for a move, I told Red I was going to go back home to live with my own family and we were going to have to break up.

My family, now consisted of my mother, brother and sister and they were sharing a house with two family friends. One was the same familiar "old family fireman friend" who had earlier guided me and the other male was my mother's new boyfriend,

---

[27] The schizophrenic may feel sad while thinking happy thoughts. Bernheim, Lewine 1979)

[28] A way through Scientology to attain greater awareness and clarity. (Awake, L. Ron Hubbard 2005)

71

J.J., a very large man and football coach. I had introduced him to my mother a few years before that and she had fallen in love with him. So, there were soon six people, including me, living in the now retired fireman's three bedroom home by the beach. It was really crowded, but I felt very safe there. Even though Red had threatened me about leaving, I knew he would be no match for the two men I would be living with, so I feared no retaliation from him.

The move was a wise decision, on my part, because my mother's renewed presence in my life would begin building my strength and self-esteem back up. It was also good to be surrounded by my family and family friends again. This latest move also represented a return to my old high school town "Port Hueneme" which I had initially felt some hesitancy about because I had almost "burned out" all of my other social, residential, and employment options in this once familiar military town at the time that I left "Sweetheart". However, at the same time, it also seemed deceptively easy to just try to throw away my problems and to form a "new beginning" there. I would experience that same false sense of security many times again before I got treatment, as I would soon come to find out.

One day, feeling a little sense of more freedom, I borrowed my mother's car and drove to the local mini-mall and a homeless person was standing just out front of the store. I gave him a quarter and, as I left, I felt a wave of turmoil and began to question my own self. Then I also heard a voice, talking in an unfamiliar way and as I left. The voice said to me in a rebuking manner, "*That was you. It could happen to you.*" I suddenly had a very terrifying thought and began to wonder "Could I end up here someday?" After all, my father had fought being homeless before and my mother almost fell victim to it three times with us while trying to survive. Sadly, my schizophrenic grandmother was also last seen as a homeless person after she became extremely ill and disappeared from her own family.

I ignored the nagging voice that something was really wrong with me and I tirelessly forced myself to stay optimistic, again, and to somehow get even a little of my confidence back. I didn't have to pay rent or work much, while I was living with my mother, so I was also able to I spend a lot of time painting. I felt, now, that I had "mastered" acrylic painting and if I just focused enough on it, I may become famous! I reminded myself that "Yes, I could - if I just worked hard enough! I was even feeling ecstatic sometimes! I worked more on my earlier art class paintings and was inspired to create more new paintings from my own original ideas. I loved painting so much and I knew my paintings were special somehow (at least they were to me) and I told myself that I had achieved exceptional levels in my works of art! I was so excited again about my many new accomplishments and it was so exciting to have a dream again. I also had an amazing amount of energy, but I realize now that I told myself these fantasies because it helped elevate me to a surreal place. Those were actually part of my extreme manic highs and delusions of grandeur.[29] These would later be diagnosed as part of my disease but were still unknown to me at the time. I knew how lucky I was to be away from the abusive relationship with Red, away from male distractions, and it was the time for me to get back to "being better" like my Mom had hoped I would. I could finally focus on my own goals and talents more, and even take art more seriously, so I continued to spend a total of four months totally committed and immersed in my own personal form of "art therapy". I also contacted a faculty member from my high school and sold a portrait of her grandchild to her which earned me a $30 dollar commission. This encouraged me that I was now on the right track.

These pleasant and comforting dreams gave me a surge of assuring endorphins. Everything was safe and comfortable for me now when it came to art and these were very real dreams. The trouble was that these also came with "manic lows." Also, at other times, my mind could not slow down. I had managed to

---

[29] The perception that one is grandiose, special, powerful or even magical (Bernhiem, Lewine 1979).

maintain my initial attraction or "affinity" (a term my Dad used from Scientology),[30] for my Spanish teacher back at Ventura College and I thought of him frequently. It helped to relax me but my feelings for him eventually became delusional when I started to believe that he was not just a teacher. I had begun to suspect that he also had a "secret" pen name and was *really* the famous woman writer Danielle Steel, my favorite romance author at the time. I also believed that he was actually a millionaire and was sending messages to me. I also believed that I could talk back with him by using my inner dialect or "broadcasting". My "inner world" continued to be something that I seemed to readily venture into, to alleviate my depression and loneliness. I didn't feel it was swallowing me up, at the time, in any way.

> *I would spend my nights, occasionally, before going to bed - on the living room couch, escaping with a now growing inner world of loneliness and helplessness. Sometimes I even really believed I could hear his voice talking back to me.*

I appreciated the attention he had given me in class and he was very friendly toward me when I was his student. I missed his class, so, one day, I confided in my mother that I really felt I needed to reach out to my Spanish teacher because I knew he really needed me because I knew something extraordinary - whether he was Danielle Steele or not.. So I went to his address, which I still had from the class party he had thrown for our class.

> *I drove there one afternoon and put a picture of myself with my phone number under his front door mat - thinking that he was really lonely and sad.*

Eventually, he called me on the phone and we went out for

---

[30] An admiration for someone. (Scientology Handbook. L. Ron Hubbard 1994).

fast food together one afternoon! It didn't turn out to be anything special between us, like I had thought it would be, and we soon lost touch. Sadly, not long afterward, he would also lose his teaching position at Ventura College and moved to another town in California to teach there. When I found myself still thinking about him, at times a few years later, I called the college where he had told me during our last visit he would be working for to inquire about him ... and I had been right. He had been desperate and despondent just like I had predicted, but it was too late by that time for us to connect. He had committed suicide!

This is one of the times when I have been able to predict unusual circumstances. My sister has always called it "my psychic powers[31]" I have always known when she was expecting a child before she has known, too.

Soon, I had accrued a collection of what I considered very successful finished paintings, but without being able to make an income with them. It was discouraging for me and suddenly I had no desire to do any more paintings. What I needed now was a job, so again, instead of seeking therapy, which I really still didn't know I needed so badly, I went back to work at the restaurant where I began my very first waitress job - at the Denny's in Port Hueneme. (This my third time working at, and then leaving Denny's, at this juncture.) I also bought a beautiful brand new car with my hard-earned, and carefully budgeted, good credit.

This time, at my old, supposedly familiar Denny's, I did not recognize any of my old friends and only recognized one or two of the customers. Not one person, not even the manager, paid much attention to me. I was also shocked that it now had become so different there. It had only been three years since I had worked there, after all. I concluded later that a lot could happen in three years *and a lot did happen*. I initially continued to uphold the belief that it would still be a great opportunity for

---

[31] Beyond known physical process (Webster's Dictionary,1990)

me regardless of the circumstances that would follow.

It was not very busy during my shifts at Denny's and I only was given about four tables in my section, instead of the usual six I thought would be allocated to me. I did manage to get all of my plates out quickly because of this, but due to the lengthy side work my station required, I didn't get all of that done in time. The whole experience soon became gloomy and very undesirable to me. "Why are all the lights so dim?" I wondered. "Why won't they talk to me?" I worried most of the time there and as a result, I was constantly "brushing off" those around me. By the third night, I worked there, I instinctively *knew* something wasn't right, but was still really shocked when without any warning, I was fired.

I felt very persecuted by "them" now and it was a real living nightmare for me that everyone there had seemed so detached and almost *sneaky* in a way. Fortunately, *since it was so frightening and weird*, I was relieved, in a way, to leave that job and not be there anymore. Not only was I still pretty young at the time, but looking back, I really feel I had been living in a total fantasy about the "real" social and workplace world – along with my place in it. No *wonder schizophrenics jump out of windows*.

I visited my father in San Diego, after that, hoping to start fresh with my life, yet another time, and to possibly live with him. I also got the chance when I went there to share my college paintings with him and even sought his own artistic touch on one of the paintings I was having a problem with. Unhappily, though, after I had gone through all the trouble and expense of driving from Ventura County all the way to San Diego on the freeway, it was not what I expected when I arrived there. I couldn't get hired on a job in San Diego, and my father was acting very impatient with me. He called my mother and told her that he wouldn't help me and that I, ultimately, needed her to intervene. For years, my father and I had always talked about making up for lost time, so I was really hurt and surprised by what he said. He also broke the lock on my little 'safe keeping' box that I had kept with me, thinking there was money in it. He *was* struggling financially and justified his actions by telling me angrily that "we don't keep secrets from one another!" Making matters worse, after I gave up and returned to Ventura County, my wonderful new car was repossessed.

Later, in 1988, my mother got enough money saved for the whole family to move into a large, charming three bedroom house with a large den and recreation room. I had found a great job working for a coffee shop, while I continued to take college classes. I really felt I was getting my life back in order and felt surprisingly "well" again. Despite this, my mother still continued to insist, over and over again, that I seek help from mental health. It was the agreement I had made in order to move back home again, but I continued to delay and ultimately refused, feeling confident, now, that I was well. I also thought that she should have more faith in me. In addition to the conflict over treatment with my mother, my brother and sister were also continually fighting with each other. I was becoming more anxious and frustrated.

It was only a few months after the move with my family to the charming house and working "successfully" at the coffee shop when I would find another "solution" that gave me new hope. I begin dating Russell, a fun, warm trustworthy, adventurous, very sweet guy who was handsome and somewhat resembled the movie idol Steve McQueen. I was now feeling adventurous about Russell *and hoping he* would start making things better for me. Soon, life suddenly did seem more promising and I felt Russell also opened a lot of doors for me at first. He owned a mobile home and seemed to really care about me, so he soon asked me to come and live with him and I enthusiastically agreed.

Russell was five years my senior, and seemingly much more mature than anyone I had ever been serious with. With him I also began to feel really normal again. He frequented the coffee shop where I worked and with my earnings I could help out and pay my own way. So, I continued to work there steadily for the three years that we were together. He introduced me to his parents and even bought me a nice necklace, a beautiful ring and a car. I didn't view his gestures to be determining factors, though, because I have never been superficial about material things. I just really enjoyed his attention. After meeting him, I would eventually undertake a challenge that would lead me to a whole new and different destination.

I did not experience any symptoms while living with Russell at all for the first two and a half years. He was a recovering alcoholic, so there was no use of alcohol or illegal drugs by either one of us. He was also an occasional smoker like I was, and we both drank a lot of coffee. I was able to keep my own job, and he eventually opened his own business right next door to the shop where I worked. There were many fun times we shared together – going to restaurants almost every night, to Las Vegas and also to San Diego where he met my Dad. We even went to a filming of "The Price Is Right" with a friend of his. I was finally content until ...

Russell would eventually surprise me when I noticed a new change in his behavior. We had always enjoyed the comfort of being together when all of a sudden after nearly three years of closeness our "happy reality" was shattered! I was at work one day when Russell and his friends came in and were enjoying some coffee when they began to tease me unexpectedly. Paramount to the discomfort of being innocently teased around his friends at the coffee shop was the fact that, due to my progressing illness, I did not feel very comfortable in the presence of groups of people and in fact, had never had felt comfortable in social situations at all, and this incident was devastating to me. It was as if all my years of illness surfaced in one awful instant!

I gave Russell and his coffee shop buddies my "brush off" coping mechanism and I believe that, at first, nothing was thought more of it on Russell's part. However, added to my own embarrassment now and lacking any good basic communication within our relationship, Russell's new behavior gave me the feeling that I didn't belong with him anymore! Not only did it change my perceptions about us, it alienated me from him. Furthermore, the sane part of me now realized that I was not "cut out" for this new more *"social"* man and this type of situation and I became very uncomfortable about this "new" Russell. I thought I had known him, but now it seemed as though he was suddenly a "mystery" to me. The truth was, though, that – secretly I was paranoid. *"Maybe he was out to get me!"* I secretly concluded about Russell.

I would eventually learn about my "group weakness" later on in therapy, and I still have those same problems today.[32] Sadly, however, due to my lack of knowledge about my progressing illness, I concluded that Russell was my new problem now. For me, at that time in my life, it was *always* somebody else's fault. This Scientology viewpoint about directing my attention at "suppressive persons" and trouble sources as the cause of my problems fit in comfortably with my own schizophrenic ideation and manner of looking at the world. I believe now that this "learned" perspective could actually be potentially dangerous for someone like me who already has paranoid tendencies to think in this manner about other people. I was completely unable to recognize my own potentially incorrect perceptions and/or delusions at that time. Also, ultimately, I think that losing so many friends and being so suspicious of their intentions and feelings about me, contributed to my own growing feelings of helplessness and hopelessness.

I tried hard to envision a life with Russell despite my judgments but I couldn't. I thought that something really terrible had happened that day and I couldn't get around it. I had also developed a somewhat dangerous secret obsession during this time period too. When things began turning out poorly in my relationship with Russell, and home videos had

---

[32] While groups are helpful in "group therapy" for schizophrenics, in real life situations they can be frightening. (Wade, 1998)

become the new rage, I began focusing my attention constantly on a famous singing sensation who I had by now become genuinely and mindlessly attracted to. I believe this may have been an unhealthy attraction but it is common for people with my illness. His real life success had a lot to do with him also being a major sex symbol, so rather than use his real name, I will call him Adonis.

I just wanted to escape the depression resulting from my own continual failings in real life so badly and wanted to think of anything else that would absorb my full attention. So, I thought of "Adonis" constantly. In truth, I knew deep down, that I couldn't reach him with my inner dialect, but I really wanted to believe I could do so because I thought, at various times, that I could hear his voice. It seemed so real sometimes. I know now that I was in such pain and so frustrated about my own life, that I was continually using my imagination to escape reality. So, Adonis was my "rock star" and my waking dream. I had found something to distract me from the loss I was feeling and with Adonis, for the first time, my "inner world" seemed to really offer me some comfort in a more consistent and consuming manner. It was truly exciting for me, at first. especially, when I contrasted it with my own actual reality.

My delusions and fantasies about "Adonis" would become very dangerous for me and they ultimately would threaten my own survival. Because of my ideations about him I would end up leaving Russell - *my real friend, the man who really loved me -* for a while during that time. I still really believed that I would somehow, in some way, meet Adonis and that we would fall in love with each other as we were really meant to do. My recent "social" disappointment and later doubts about Russell had also taken a toll on me and I started to feel confused and anxious again, I wanted so much to be self-sufficient and to take care of myself and began to suspect, again, that it was perhaps actually the city I was living in that was holding me back. So, for a brief time, I went to live at the Church of Scientology organization in Los Angeles in order to escape.

The Church of Scientology was better known by major media as a cult at that time, but because of my father's lifelong devotion to Scientology I had obviously never thought of it that way. My father had even lived at Saint Hill in England as a young man and been taught directly by L. Ron Hubbard in classes there. He treasured his class notes and personal moments with Hubbard and Mary Sue, his devoted wife. He had worked for the Washington D.C. Organization when it was raided by the government, but he zealously considered Scientology's wisdom beyond reproach. He loved the founder L. Ron Hubbard and saw Scientology as the solution for everything ... so, I was very surprised to find out that my new adventure and search for a solution - for me - at the Church of Scientology in Los Angeles was not at all like I thought it would be. I would begin to feel very paranoid while I was there as well.

There was also a big cafeteria there where we all ate. There were daily exercise drills and Scientology classes, along with daily chores we all had to do there, so I cleaned a lot of bathrooms. I slept in a room with two other beds and other girls. I had very few possessions with me, which included a big portrait of "Adonis" a beautiful pencil drawing I had created to give to him when we met ...

I was terrified of everyone at the Organization. They all seemed so secretive - like people had during my gloomy experience at Denny's.

I started to just look out the window longingly at all the night-time city lights and yearn for a real life and freedom from what I still believed at the time had been very unfortunate relationships.

A very concerned and seemingly nurturing lady tried to take me under her wing by telling me she "would protect me and not let anyone hurt me" at the Church of Scientology, but her efforts didn't help ...

The religion that I respected so highly and the very helpfulness I had always received did not light

the way for me anymore ...
    What was the way?

I soon realized that it wasn't the city I lived in that had been holding me back - *it was "me."*

I called my father and told him that I felt out of place in this uncomfortable situation and asked him if he could come get me.

He said he couldn't, but told me, instead, that it was just a *"3-D Thing"*. The Third Dynamic or "3-D" is a term used in Scientology to identify a group social situation.[33]

After trying to stay there a little longer, I was finally able to leave after calling Russell to come and get me. When he arrived, I was thankful that Russell *did* come and that the Church actually let me leave, but I still didn't want to stay with Russell anymore. I desperately wanted to break up with him and I now suspected that he was hiding something strange from me but I couldn't figure out what it was. By this time, Russell did not seem really affected by my wanting to leave, either - his thoughts seemed to be saying to me *"Whatever"* ...

When we actually started breaking up, I became really depressed but it wasn't so much about Russell at first. I think I was just angry and depressed about my uncertain future and total lack of emotional stability. I wanted so much to show others that I could succeed and live like an independent successful young woman, have a good job, and not always be the subject of scrutiny. Then, at other times, I would believe that it had really been just Russell who was holding me back. I was convinced now that *he was the "root " of my problem* - and this was that same awful thinking and behavior pattern that had led me to continue "disconnecting" from all of my friends in the past. I always felt that it was *"them"* and that I was really truly okay when I disconnected from someone. Yet, now - more than at any other time - I felt extreme guilt about breaking ties with Russell as a result of my Scientology beliefs. I was just still so

---

[33] Advance! magazine scientology, 2015

influenced, at the time, by my father's very assertive viewpoints about Scientology and "SP"s (suppressive people) - and by my own delusional beliefs that others were "against me".

My mother began to insist *again* that I go to a psychiatrist, so I finally reluctantly agreed to do so. I made an appointment at the local Mental Health Clinic which was, in no way, easy for me to do because of all the preaching and warnings about Psychiatry from my father, as well as from my many readings and recent classes in Scientology. I feared that my father would be extremely angry with me and perhaps even "disconnect"[34] from me - or decide I had become someone he would no longer desire to share wonderful times with. In the past, my father had always been so proud of me and I didn't want to lose that relationship with him. I was also very resistant to even ask for professional mental health services, because I was still convinced nothing serious was wrong with me. Yet, at the same time, I couldn't ignore the fact that it was getting progressively really hard for even me to evaluate myself on a consistent basis anymore.

I felt now that my state of mind often fluctuated somewhat erratically depending on who I surrounded myself with at different times and upon how much stress I was under. Also significant at the time was that several of my ongoing symptoms, along with my recurrent paranoia and delusional thinking, were completely non-apparent to myself and to others during less stressful moments in my life. Nonetheless, despite all of my resistance and excuses not to - I finally took that first step and called for help. Then, I followed up and attended my first appointment.

I didn't say much during my initial sessions, but now that I was finally in therapy, I was calm, cool, collected, and reserved for the first few months. I was certain that going to mental

---

[34] To completely end all relations with someone. (Scientology Handbook L. Ron Hubbard 1994)

health would just be a "stepping stone" for me and that I would prove my mother - and everyone else - wrong. I was also at the same time, even *more eager* to prove to myself and to others that I could still work and support myself and become independent- and that was a good reason for me to go there – and maybe even a good reason to *keep going.* [35]

> " ... *In a sense , at first, I felt I was in an uncomfortable position ... pursuing the avenue of Mental Health would mean something was wrong. I didn't want anything to disrupt my learned coping mechanism of "positive thinking", but finally deciding to go there would turn out to be best decision I ever made. Without the intervention of family members I may not have gotten the help I needed ...*"

---

[35] "Work magically transforms a patient into a person, Patients will often work very hard to control their psychiatric symptoms while working." Furthermore Torrey states, "Work provides a daily structure, a reason to get out of bed in the morning, an identity and an extended social network." (Torrey, 2001)

Wise Owl (1988)

I continued to tell myself that it was good for me to be going to mental health and good that I had taken my mother's advice, even though things were not perfect yet, by any means... (p. 95)

Mysterious Forces **(2012)**

"I soon found out that "The FACE" would come back worse during stress and/or when neglecting my medication, I was falling into an abyss ... I was really a freak. My life was now completely falling apart ...".

CHAPTER SIX

Falling

In 1992, I was tested at mental health and talked briefly, at first, to a therapist. My therapist was a very tall woman with a pleasant personality and she accepted me right from the start. I would begin seeing my tall therapist once a week. As my first therapist, she was perfect and I felt right at home with her at times. Truthfully, I was still wondering if she could really help me at all, because I was still listening to my father and believed in my own coping mechanism of "positive thinking" as the perfect solution. Sometimes, and surprisingly so - I found, that it really was great to talk about all my thoughts and feelings to someone who seemed compassionate. At the time, I was still often engaged in broadcasting my thoughts and imagining that my favorite singer "Adonis" was receiving them, so I felt I was really sharing something out of the ordinary with her and happy to have someone listening. On the other hand, after some of her reactions, I ended up feeling clownish, "out of place" and somewhat ridiculous. I entertained the thought that I was probably very amusing to my therapist her as I told her about my delusions. She seemed very nice and just listened to me which would eventually make me feel more committed to the support I was getting. On the other hand, I felt like she was not offering me any quick solutions or handy answers for why I was there.

I was now under another slowly rising type of pressure, just trying to keep going to therapy, and to keep communicating, constantly, without any input or conversation from my new therapist. Our therapy sessions involved a lot of me talking about my problems which was "not positive" at all in my own mind, and was also awkward for me. It felt very unnatural to me to talk about my negative ideas and feelings to someone else and, unlike talking to my father or my mother, to have no answers or ideas being offered to me. I would sense later on in treatment that, maybe, in contrast to all of my other future therapists, my tall beautiful first therapist had been the most sympathetic and understanding person even though I know that at first she was suspicious of me. Then, after only a couple months or so, my therapist surprised me. She told me that I also needed to see a psychiatrist and I KNEW instantly that this meant DRUGS because they are medical doctors, too. In the beginning, I had been really afraid of seeing a psychiatrist at the Mental Health Clinic because of my fear of taking mind-altering DRUGS and I hadn't met with one yet – but now, my therapist was requiring me to see one. The casual feeling I had about our sessions was now fully over! I was extremely frightened ... *"They were going to do me in!"*

My therapist offered to "sit in" with me while seeing the psychiatrist and I felt I had to go along with she was suggesting. So, I would meet my psychiatrist for the first time with my therapist right alongside me. He was a man in his early 40's, kindly, enthusiastic, and bubbly - and I soon wondered why I was afraid to meet him after all. Sitting in his office for the first time, I also began wondering why they were "stepping it up" this way now - *insisting* that I consider medication! It was no longer light hearted anymore. In a way, I felt like maybe they DID know something was wrong. This kind doctor was the other side of me, the side of me that felt "right"' and "well". One part of me wanted to tell him all about everything that was right about me, but the other side of me was afraid that, if I did, he would decide that I was "alright" and *that would be it!* My visits with him would be over and I struggled with these conflicting feelings throughout therapy. I didn't want either the psychiatrist or my therapist to desert me and I also wanted to somehow earn their respect.

I wanted to come out of this "positive" and to end this chapter of my life feeling victorious. However, in another way, I suspiciously thought my psychiatrist was just unnecessarily trying to medicate anyone he could get his hands on! I was still somewhat negative about psychiatry, of course, because of all of my father's preaching. Yet, I had also worked successfully quite a few times in my life, so I also feared they might be suspicious of me, too, that I could be deceiving them! If I sometimes couldn't think of anything to say in my psychiatrist's office I felt all the more deceptive. I felt stupid as *a firm believer in scientology* and also guilty. I struggled with speechlessness around my psychiatrist often. If all I could think of, during a session, was my crazy fantasies about "Adonis," and I *knew* by this time they were fantasies, therefore, why bring them up? I also would go blank, or unable to remember all of my symptoms, and was often stupefied. I was not yet aware of the state my brain was actually existing in and the dulled emotions that made me so "undesirable" as a person socially. I was also not aware of some of the other symptoms as being important except for my occasional "voices" which I hadn't heard as much in the past three years.

Significantly, before therapy, I had always thought that other people also heard voices too. At this time, my voices were also somewhat under control because of the fantasy "Adonis" escape. Deep down, I knew I needed mental health treatment, but I was just really confused - pulled in all different directions. Therefore, my early attempts at therapy and at obtaining medication were half-hearted at the beginning. I ultimately felt like that by seeking their help, the *real truth* would finally come out - that I *was really mentally alright* - and then I suddenly decided that the *real problem* was nothing serious – I was just a loser! Nevertheless, despite my persistent denials, as time went on, I slowly began to resist treatment less and became more cooperative. Even then, as I cooperated more and tried to be an ideal patient, my struggles to successfully regain my life, comply with treatment and to find and adjust to the proper medication for me were not totally over. My own experimentation with the pills could be somewhat dangerous at this time for me too, as everyone around me would soon find out.

My psychiatrist tried four different medications in total

throughout treatment for me. The first antidepressant Trazadone, worked a little for a while. During that time period, I would always experiment briefly with a suggested drug regimen, then stop quickly, because I didn't like the side effects or trust that it was a good solution for someone like me. All and all, the medications prescribed at the time, were a good distraction at first. I would even occasionally feel more comfortable in therapy sessions because of taking the medicines and begin to reveal more life experiences to my therapist. When I did that, I would sometimes feel a little surprised at the results. I was beginning to feel a bit more "normal" and slowly also began to feel stronger and comfortable with myself. *I really wanted to be truthful* with those I spoke with at mental health, *at least* for the most part, which I think was good. I talked to them about my problems with other females and about my fantasy rocker, "Adonis." My tall therapist told me that he probably reminded me of someone and she was right. His smile had an ever so slight resemblance to "Sweetheart's" and there was something in his eyes as well.

I also talked to her about my relationship with Russell, who had been my most recent "living situation" at the time. I was very open with her about my feeling of alienation and estrangement from him. She always seemed very interested in what I said and she was a great listener. I told her about my father, my family, past relationships and work situations. I also told her that I always wanted to feel respected and that I was often getting into relationships that turned out very badly. I admitted to her that, even in pleasant situations, like going to the swap meet, years ago, with "Sweetheart," I always felt that I really needed to be somewhere else.

My tall therapist told me during one session that I was attempting to gain control of all my *"wild horses"* a phrase that I really didn't completely understand until much later. When I eventually began to gain additional insights about my "inner world" from talking with her, I came to conclude that I really had been experiencing a lot of fleeting dreams and distractions in my everyday life. At the time, these had actually become more dominant in my mind than any of my "real life" situations and activities. In retrospect, it seems as if my mind and energy were always "stuck" in a situation, with those "wild horses" perpetually surrounding me - dreams in motion, all around me - boldly running away with my psyche. She was right. *I really was trying to gain control of them.*

I continued to tell myself that it was good for me to be going to mental health and good that I had taken my mother's advice, even though things were not perfect yet, by any means. I had a *reason* to be there even though the psychiatrist's attempts, according to my own perspective, were proving ineffective, overall, for two full years during my early treatment. I was still hoping to get some good advice from therapy sessions, but I didn't seem to get as much "actual *practical* advice" about my life as I wanted. I was still having problems with many other workplace and social situations. I still wasn't completely in present time. I also *still* wasn't asserting myself with other people.

This, I would learn later, was because when I first began therapy I did not want just "be present" and talk to someone or to assert myself much of the time. Doing that would interfere with my constant escape into obsessing. Even more frightening, it could possibly release the anger that was always flooding through me frequently at some level. I was angry at what I still considered a "questionable" situation at mental health and at my own deteriorating social status. Looking back, that is my own self-diagnosis. I just kept trying to "think positive", and I know now that if I had not received professional help things could have been a whole lot worse for me.

My psychiatrist was also causing me a tremendous amount of anxiety. I felt *too normal* around him sometimes. He was constantly trying to get me on the right medication, which in one respect, I resented. Yet, in another respect, I actually wanted to find out for myself if something would work for me. *I did want* something to take the *"edge "* off my anxiety and fear as well as to help me live better after meeting him. "Who doesn't want that?" I thought guiltily. At times, I felt he might have thought that *maybe I should just go have a drink!* I panicked a lot, and I even sometimes exaggerated to him - telling him the voices were *constantly* there, at first, when, actually, they were not always there *all the time.* I told him this, though, to maintain a reason for being there, even though I was at war inside my mind about going or not going to Mental Health.

It took me a long time to really develop some trust with him. I didn't know it then, but I later found out that he was in continual communication with my Tall Therapist. I guess that's why they call them a mental health team. He knew all along all of my crazy delusions or at least he *had* to have known, or he may have refused to see me any longer. As time went by, I suspected that perhaps some of my own fears and failed attempts at compliance may have caused him to be as suspicious of me, as I was of him. After all, I was secretly avoiding becoming too reliant on any medications but, overall, still doing somewhat better. In addition, I had become more able to successfully avert the root of my terror - "The FACE" - at that time. Yet, I was still continually engaged in a very uncomfortable balancing act. By this time, I was certain that the only thing I could feel comfortable about or really do well in, was art.

My mother was worrying constantly about me by this time, but I continued to maintain a relationship with her and with other family members. Meanwhile, I hesitantly made the slow, painful, move out of my disintegrating relationship with Russell. We had now been living together only for convenience and any hope for our continued relationship was over. My sister, who had become a single teenage mother at a very young age, helped me a lot at this time, too. She needed family support from me at the time, just like I did from her. We went to Disneyland and on walks together with her baby in the stroller and my life slowly became more "normal". I began to reach out socially again. My brother, who was nineteen, by this time, had formed a band, so I went to his nightclub gigs. Unfortunately, I came out of a club one time very drunk - I had taken my antidepressant, earlier that day and got really sick when I returned to Russell's mobile home.

My sister may have saved my life that day. She rushed to my side and, along with my mom, and helped get me into the tub to "sober up". I just kept repeating to them how I was going to meet Adonis, my imaginary celebrity friend. My mother was even more frightened about my well-being now and I would soon flee from Russell's both humiliated and failed by him. I had hoped we could live together peacefully but it was now very uncomfortable just to be around him. In addition, we could not communicate and he did not have one single artistic quality, in any form, which I felt I wanted in a partner at that point. I broke all of my former ties with Russell and even quit my job at the coffee shop next to his store, where I had been working for three years.

I know now that Russell was really not a bad person at all , but that my own ego and or what I sometimes now refer to as my delusions of grandeur (described earlier) were really getting in our way. Despite going to mental health, trying different medications, and avoiding "The Face", I had begun to have more delusions of grandeur, during my time with him. I believed that my dad was, in secret, a songwriter who wrote songs that were played on the radio. It seemed quite possible, since my father was a painter and writer and he had even had an article published in a major Seattle newspaper once. I also thought that twenty five other songs on the radio were being sung just for me. Yet, sadly, despite my lofty delusions of fame celebrity and fortune, life in the real world continued – and my own constant struggle to survive went on.

I rented a room from an elderly lady named Dorothy whom I had met once at a temporary job. At first, I enjoyed the pressures and challenges my new freedom and new room presented for me. I was able to pay my rent there and take care of myself successfully for about seven months. In the beginning stages, everything went so fast. I managed to get three different part-time jobs that I was initially very proud of, and I used those jobs to pay rent and buy food. One of my jobs was working at a liquor store, but I lost it right away because I was not "the liquor store type". The other two were low-paying fast-food jobs, but strangely enough, I managed to hold on to them, for a while, then quit them, on my own, later on.

I think that my new relative success at the workplace may have been due to being in therapy, and to taking my medication, although I was seldom consistent about it. During that time, I actually began to think that I was now "alright" and just needed to keep my remaining steady jobs. In my personal life, the mysterious and enchanting fantasy "Adonis" was not only a great romantic singer but he also wrote music as well. I related to him, as a fellow artist, but I now also really wanted to follow my dream now to be with him romantically. Could this famous celebrity really actually be my true soul mate? The one who I would share a similar ARC (affinity, reality and communication) like my dad described in terms from Scientology?[36] I also thought that a powerful dream and ultimate connection like that would make me even more determined to succeed in my life.

I had ideas a mile long, at that juncture, about everything in life. I remembered my dad's philosophy about "'being an artist'" and also Scientology's view about what it meant to be an artist. I had always been such an *observer* had become so philosophical, exactly like my Dad was. I really wanted to see "Adonis" again in concert. I was very comforted in my dreams about him now and growing more and more curious about him. I wanted to find out now if there was any indication that *he was really my destiny*. Since I believed that maybe it was possible that Adonis was receiving my magical thoughts on some level, I decided to ask a male co-worker from one of my fast food jobs

---

[36] Scientologists refer to a theorem called the "ARC Triangle". At the top of the triangle is Affinity. On both sides at the bottom are Reality and Communication. Communication is the most important part, in essence, opening the door for Affinity and Reality.

into taking me to Orange County to see him for the fourth time in a concert. He told me he would drop me off, but not take me home, which seemed reasonable enough to me.

I only had one ticket to the Adonis concert and no friends to go with but I had already gone to three of his performances when I was with Russell and during the time right afterward. At the second concert I attended, I had even given him a big, beautiful portrait I had done of him in pencil. I remember being somewhat hurt that evening because when I handed it to him, he smiled at me, but his smile wasn't what I expected it to be. I would later comfort myself with the thought that at least I got to give it to him personally. Now, this time I just wanted to see "Adonis" so badly, again and was so grateful that I was really going to see him ...

I thought that maybe I would be lucky enough to be sitting in a front row of a concert, and Adonis would put me on the stage and we would live happily ever after ...

Obviously, that never happened. I was so young, only 23, and in the grasp of serious mental illness and a lot was about to happen to me in the years to come. After my final Adonis concert was over that evening, I ended up stranded in Orange County, alone, in the large empty stadium parking lot, nearly a hundred miles away from home at 10:00 o'clock at night. I began walking in the dark looking for a Denny's so I could hang out there all night until the train station would be open. How would I get home now? While I was walking in the dark, before I even had the chance to consider hitch hiking, three cheerful, nice Hispanic men pulled up and offered to drive me all the way back home to Port Hueneme! I was lucky that I decided to trust this young, seemingly sincere, group. They were safe – and when they dropped me off, many miles later, at my room in Dorothy's home, I thanked them. They even gave me their phone number but I never called them. Many years later, my mother still gets wide-eyed and breathes a sigh of relief when we talk about that

95

night and what could have happened to me.

My wonderful concert experience with my dream fantasy man "Adonis" was now over, and my remaining fast food jobs continued to provide me with the money I needed for my responsibilities. My jobs also kept me sane. After, all, stress at the workplace had become a major hindrance for me in life, but I still kept those particular fast food jobs for a long time to come. I did experience some problems, though, and one job became particularly stressful because another female co-worker there started harassing me again. Then, on another job, my "super-human health genes" failed me (I suspect due to my coffee drinking habit) and I began to get bad pelvic pains. I left work to rush to the emergency hospital for treatment and got my hours cut as a result. I was left with only a mere eight hour week at one job, which meant that I might not now even be able to pay my rent. Worse still, I had already been forced to apply for food stamps in order to buy food.

I still remained optimistic about being on my own and away from Russell but, unfortunately, would soon begin having problems at my little room rental which I still called my "home" at this point. In my rush to obtain housing, I had not taken time to get to know the older lady landlord/roommate that well before I rented from her. I would find out before long that she had a troubling and serious heart condition. That made me very anxious and I would soon become delusional about my new roommate. I began to experience a continually developing fear that she could hear my thoughts just like I had felt when I lived with the Amway landlords when I first graduated from high school. I expressed my new fears about living with there with the elderly lady to my mother so she visited us in order to meet her. They talked together for a while and my mother seemed to like her personality so I felt a little less frightened and uncomfortable living there.

By this time, my mother had moved to a nice apartment on the other side of town with a new boyfriend. He was nice and she seemed happy with him, so I would often ride my bike to go and visit them. I felt totally free on my bicycle, loving the exercise and what I perceived of as a new beginning. *At that time I actually was beginning to feel comfortable living within my intense and sometimes exhilarating existence.* This may sound surprising, but I especially liked the feeling when I sometimes would stop taking my medication. I felt more "alive" that way, and I just wanted above all to stay happy with myself. I would feel as if I was "playing hooky" from school or something. I later read that resisting medication is common for those with my disease.

On the other hand, I would sometimes try faithfully to stick with my medication knowing deep down that it was probably best for me to do so. Then, on one visit with my mother, when I attempted to "show off" my new personality on a new antidepressant I was taking, I felt that this "new me" was rejected by my mother and, at first, I was extremely resentful about her reaction of this "me". I have never wanted to have conflicts with my mother, so I just "turned the other cheek" after her response, but I was still very disappointed about her reaction to my new "functioning" personality.

Apparently, I learned later after we became much closer, as mother and daughter, that she actually felt that I was not still not consistently taking my illness seriously and getting better. In her eyes, I still had that superficial façade, at times, which she has always reacted negatively to and been firm about her dislike of and convictions about.

I was also getting bored now most of the time and television was becoming more difficult for me to focus on.[37] Just trying to watch TV quietly in my rented room, *was often a nightmare* so I escaped my home situation by accessing "studio space" at a friend of the family's commercial building. I was attempting to create some great art again and was comfortable there at first.

---

[37] Symptoms such as voices and depression can make it hard for a schizophrenic to focus and concentrate (Torrey, 2001).

After a while though, my paintings were harder for me to render due to complications with my medication for depression, a drug called Trazadone[38] At the same time, *the art I began to create at the office space was causing me to believe that my elderly roommate Dorothy might be receiving a curse originating from my attempts to rid myself of obsessive thoughts.* Often times, the bicycle ride back home from the office space to Dorothy's room was terrifying and I would experience a sensation that felt as if I was falling from "space".

I soon also developed persistent "blackouts,'" which I later learned were caused by my "off and on" attempts to take Trazadone. Now, after only a week of trying to escape into creativity and that not working, I wondered to myself what I should do! I decided to try to take my medication more responsibly and to pray that the increasingly powerful delusions would stop. My "rational" mind was idle - except for my prayers - much of the time. Despite my efforts to comply with medication, I was also having poor results from Trazadone and began screaming in my sleep in the middle of the night, even though I didn't seem to fully realize my own waking fears most of the time. As a result, since my roommate was elderly, I was finally informed by her that I had to find another room to rent. Her heart condition was being aggravated by my screaming at night and, although perhaps it shouldn't have, this came as a big shock to me.

I was now also having longer blackouts and frequent panic attacks so I felt that I really needed my mother to intervene. However, Dorothy had made up her mind already and I had to move again. The last thing I wanted to do was go back to Russell, even though it would have provided security for me. I now felt even more pressure and anxiety about being forced to get to know and live with a new prospective roommate.

First, I had to look in the newspaper and the only good

---

[38] Marked diminution of creativity and spontaneity have been reported as side effects due to medication therapy (Torrey,2001)

room was on the other side of town. I called the phone number for the rental ad and a very worried voice was on the other end of the line. His name was George and he was 47 years old, very polite, respectful and - I would later find out - also a recovered alcoholic. After our initial meeting, when I left his residence, I immediately felt uneasy and unbalanced despite his congeniality. I wasn't sure that I wanted to rent this prospective new room until my mother came with me for a second look to approve of it. My possible new landlord/roommate seemed to open up to my mother, so she approved of him fondly, and I moved in right away. George was very quiet at first, so we just watched TV together for a couple nights. It seemed we were both afraid to talk to one other. Then, I wasn't living there for long before his old roommate Janet called, wanting to move back in. Since George had three rooms, that's what she ended up doing.

There *were not* a lot of positive things to reflect upon when I first moved in with George and my illness was about to come to a precipice and become more severe at this heedless time. Janet seemed like she might become a great friend for me at first. She was pretty, with a big smile, and it was exciting to possibly have her as a new friend. However, right from the start, she avoided eye contact with me and I did the same with her. It was also very awkward because George and Janet began to "hang out" a lot and they would pick me up from my job together. It seemed like a nice gesture at first, but Janet soon became vindictive towards me, seemingly for no reason I could think of. George reassured me that she did that to everyone so I tried to adjust but I grappled with it.

I expressed feelings at mental health about living there with both of them and not being able to communicate with Janet. I explained to my therapist, during one session, that I had tried to respond to Janet's first friendly "Hello", but then soon felt nervous and lost my functions. I just couldn't turn off the unpleasant tones, or "grab hold" of any happy tones which was the reason I couldn't look at her. My emotions were continually "fleeting" and my inability to filter unwanted emotions, also called my "faulty filter",[39] caused very frightening interactions with Janet. Since George and Janet were going to Alcoholics Anonymous meetings and watching television together all the time, I was also a little jealous of their relationship and, before long, I decided that I really didn't like the situation of living there with them anymore. My father had also told me during a recent conversation that he would not speak to me as long as I was seeing a psychiatrist which complicated everything in my life even more.

After only a week or so, of feeling left out and troubled at George's house, I considered a new option when I encountered Adele, a Filipino saleslady I originally met when working at Bob's Big Boy, in the supermarket. She had a nice four bedroom house and offered to let me stay with her. I reluctantly accepted and moved in with Adelle and her family. I stayed in her daughter's room which I felt really guilty about and it was also very crowded there. In addition to her own children, her husband and her father, a friendly middle-aged close friend of their family was also renting a room there. He soon became very persistent about trying to get me to go out with him and I wasn't very happy about that. I really just wanted him to leave me alone. I began tearing up pictures, smoking more "off" and "on", and just wanted to use up some of my excess energy. I would end up staying at Adele's for about two months and then began looking for another place.

I was still going to see my therapist and psychiatrist at Mental Health, but not taking it seriously enough, I still thought that, since I was able to get jobs and work somewhere, I was really okay. I was still only about 5 or 6 months into treatment and I wasn't really feeling the urgency and stress yet of getting well yet. The Trazadone still wasn't working and, as they continued to assess treatment alternatives for me, I didn't know that by now they were actually taking my condition VERY

---

[39] The term "faulty filter" was described earlier in Chapter 5

seriously. So, despite my hesitation and fear of trying a second medication, my psychiatrist was now insisting that I try Mellaril, a mild antipsychotic. I actually did feel some comfort when I took it - especially because it seemed to ease the threat of "The FACE" that always hung over me. All of my "voices" were also still there though – in "Mellaril" tones.

I would continue taking Mellaril for a while and then stopped but, after some time, I asked my psychiatrist if I could use the drug again because it had come the closest to any at alleviating my unbearable anxiety. My psychiatrist didn't like that idea and told me that I couldn't just stop medication and then try it again later, but he did allow me to do so for a short while. My psychiatrist also wanted to increase the Mellaril dosage during that time, but I didn't want to take a larger dose of it or take it for too long. I shared my concerns with him, explaining that I was afraid of taking too much because of my father's constant warnings. Looking back, I realize now that my father's influence on me made it extremely difficult for the doctor to prescribe medication and treat me appropriately for my symptoms. Since I knew my father would not approve of what I was doing at mental health in order to try and get well - knowing that was the most painful part all along.

Surprisingly, I think that my efforts to comply and take my Mellaril at that time, did help me create some impressive art at Adelle's house! I also took on an additional Christmas job at a retail store, in addition to the last fast food job I still had. The latest job turned out to be only "seasonal" and the New Year found me very low on funds and also very disappointed. By this time, I also had no reliable car and was still riding my bike for transportation. My mother remained hopeful that I would eventually get the right treatment and felt I was, at least, learning some things about my condition that she had been trying to teach me all along. At the same time, she also recognized that my mental and job instability was beginning to have a very negative impact on my survival and housing needs. I already diligently tried and failed at so many jobs by this time, that she and my sister began to suggest I obtain "help" for my "disability" on a regular basis. At this point, I had come to believe that I was actually, in truth, too strong, too capable, and too high-functioning to apply for more social services, mental health services or to even consider receiving social security for disabled persons, so I refused to agree with them. In fact, I even felt stupid for going to Mental Health in the first place.

It just had begun to feel as if I was 'beating an old horse into the ground" and the effort was, for the most part, still entirely meaningless. I wrote to my father not mentioning anything about mental health or medication at first and suddenly it seemed as if we were on speaking terms again! He told me that I could come and live with him, but to "travel light" and not bring a lot of my belongings with me. I will always remember him telling me that, because I was so shocked to hear those words and, in fact, was also very leery about his invitation at this point. He, too, was always having bouts with his own homelessness, so I sensed that, realistically, maybe moving with him would not be a good, permanent solution for me either - even though I had always been so excited to see him during all of our happy years as father and daughter. He had always lifted my spirits when I was with him and I always felt good afterward, especially during that time I visited him with Russell in San Diego. Yet, I did recognize now that learning to "live with my illness" was becoming a serious endeavor – one that was beginning to cause me to wander from the safe path my father had once paved for me.

I did not stay with him in San Diego and my Scientologist father and I would go on not seeing each other for the three year time period that followed. I was now painfully aware of all the negative aspects of his nature at this time in my life when I felt especially sensitive and was questioning everything in my life. It also became significant to me that my father would never choose to give up drinking if his life depended on it. My father even proudly stated to me on numerous occasions that he only "*used* alcohol" as if he had figured a way to exist without any implications from it.

Luckily, by now, I was still working at one of my remaining jobs and receiving a general relief rent voucher so I was actually able to pay for a new room to rent. I started wishing things had worked out better with George for my own housing and stability needs, even though I was, deep down, really frustrated about what happened when Janet moved in. I called George back, hoping that maybe she had moved out – and she had! George immediately came and got me and I noticed the smell of alcohol in his car on the way to his house. I began to wonder for a moment about my latest desperate choice, but I tried not to worry. I was just grateful to move back in his house with him, but he shocked me by getting really angry at me shortly after I moved back in! He unexpectedly shouted at me for no apparent reason. I remember very well that I had done nothing but to just walk past him! The dizziness I felt when that happened, along with my sudden extreme incapacitation was something I will never forget! I don't think George even began to realize the impact that moment had on me.

I know now that my helpless reaction was due, again, to my unsuccessful medication regimen compliance. I still wasn't taking my Mellaril on a structured schedule. In addition, I didn't realize the ultimate consequences, again, of not standing up for myself. I just immediately began to adjust to George's temperament because I was no stranger to people with what I perceived of as volatile temperaments, for instance my parents, getting upset with me for what seemed like no reason at all. As I got to know George better, thankfully, similar sudden outbursts on his part didn't happen much after that. On the positive side, he was a hardworking electrician and well over 100 pounds overweight but still very dynamic and attractive. He had a fantastic, even brilliant sense of humor, despite his occasional bad temper. A full nineteen years older than I was, George was also a lot more relaxed and mature than my other boyfriends had been in the past.

I soon became romantically interested in him and drawn to

a certain charisma he had. Caring for him became natural for me, although I did continue, at first, to have some reservations and trust issues with him because of his anger and food issues. As time went on, I would realize that George was also prone to be *more hostile* at certain times. For example, he would shout obscenities at others on occasion and I knew this was wrong to do, so it would make me become uncomfortable. Feeling helpless, I just searched for answers from God and prayed that He would change his behavior or give me the strength to endure it.

Janet still came around the house to visit, occasionally, but after a while, there was a big argument between she and George and, to my relief, she was permanently gone. I later ran into a friend of Janet's and she was quick to inform me that "George was a very sick man". I listened, but I actually came to feel over time that maybe George wasn't that bad after all and that her remarks were probably a scheme to get him and Janet back together. I also learned an unsettling fact, after knowing George for some time - that *George's wife had earlier fled from him leaving all of her possessions behind!* Yet, despite finding all of this out, I intuitively felt there was really no other solution for my everyday survival than to stay with George – *and above all* - I now loved him.

Despite my devotion, I would sometimes begin to really question myself and feel trapped. I was afraid to try to convey an air of confidence around George ever since the first shouting incident. I told myself to "sulk" for a while, an idea supported by a little voice in my head. It was now my father's voice – sometimes - telling me what to do during those types of uneasy situations. I appeared to be compliant, but I was also confused. If I ever felt "well" and unsuspecting and George had shouted at me again, I felt I would be devastated and "finished" so to speak, so I continued to act submissive and also very guarded throughout the years I would live with him. I believe that George eventually came to distrust that "personality" and it may have even made him worry that I would leave him in the future, since it soon seemed as if I would be guarded around him - all of the time.

Mellaril eventually stopped working altogether. I told my psychiatrist and was advised to try Navane which is another mild antipsychotic drug. It didn't take any of the edge off of my anxiety so I told my psychiatrist right away that it didn't work at all and stopped using it. Now with bottles of pills that didn't work and all the confusion about what to do, my blackouts were making me really dizzy and frenzied, all at the same time, and I soon began screaming at night at George's house too. After he had exploded at me for what seemed like no reason, it seemed like everything, not only between us, but in the world around me had changed. I thought that maybe I was going to lose my job due to my changing inner dialect after that outburst and I was right. After that, I had my first major setback and everything I had been trying to establish at mental health - my confidence, gracefulness, natural friendliness and unsuspecting nature would very soon become a thing of the past.

One day I was obsessing about George and trying really hard to keep my own private "evil voices" from reaching what I imagined to be his own private thoughts. I was frightened that I was in such a scary, weird, state of mind and I was also really terrified of being "found out". I thought that I had now, for the most part, become a stranger to myself and to others in my life as well. I struggled with an overwhelming shame over what I felt were my usually ineffective and *bad* coping mechanisms. I was also battling with a brand new symptom of schizophrenia. Now, I was not only hearing my own thoughts spoken to me, but the last words of a thought were now being repeated in an evil voice that I did not recognize. I felt overwhelming estrangement from the real present circumstances I was in and I could sense that something had somehow turned terribly wrong for me. I wasn't going to be able to keep a job at all while I was continually broadcasting evil voices with my mind anymore. It was *really serious now*, and I was *now* becoming even more terrified. I was getting ready to leave for work on my bicycle and I started having, for the first time what I know now was a serious, totally uncontrollable panic attack.[40]

I suddenly knew that I had no control of myself at all anymore and that I had to quit my only remaining job! I also would realize later that my panic attack as I was leaving for work was really a plea to somehow, in some way, to *really assert myself - somehow, somewhere, and to someone, sometime in my life!*

I woke up the following morning in a *sad, dismal* mood after quitting my last remaining successful job. Despite my success at managing to exist in my new "rooming" arrangement with George, I suddenly felt distressed and severely victimized. I was also really scared with no job to rely upon. I was also terrified that maybe, with no income, I would not ever even be able to keep the rent for my room paid. I also now felt as if I was quickly losing the ability to appear functional and "normal" in public. It seemed as if some "higher" power that I once had was now gone. Every voice that interfered with my daily life caused me more pain. *Was I just so uncontrollably angry because I didn't have what others had?*

I kept my broadcasting a complete secret in my everyday life. I still would keep my doctor appointments and I tried to keep everything I was experiencing under control in my home life, but it was, in a sense, like living in darkness. It was now as if George was on an entirely different planet from me and I just wanted to get there with him somehow. Above and beyond all, I now thought that the only thing I really wanted was a simple life.

My mother turned out to be the only light at the end of the tunnel during those days. I had also begun, slowly, to really have a change of heart toward her after going to Mental Health. My mother and I would surprisingly become even more close when I noticed more how much she still cared about me throughout

---

[40] A panic attack is a sudden urge of overwhelming anxiety or fear. The heart rate goes up and breathing is difficult. Sometimes it is accompanied by the feeling that the sufferer is going crazy or dying. (Web MD 2015).

everything that kept happening. My situation was very distressing to her but, even though I was not totally following the program at Mental Health at the beginning, I think she at least felt there was some hope and, therefore, became less anxious about me. Headstrong and strong-willed, my mother had suffered a very tragic past. Her own mother, my grandmother, Lily, who was a schizophrenic herself, raised my mother for as long as she could, then deserted her. There wasn't much treatment for schizophrenia in those days – primarily shock treatment and lobotomies. Shortly after losing her mother to schizophrenia, she lost her father to cancer, after nursing his frail body for six months, and was placed in an orphanage.

The last time my mother saw her own mother was right before her high school graduation. Lily was homeless and crossing the street near Pershing Square in downtown Los Angeles. When my mother approached her mother, hoping to tell her about her upcoming graduation, Lily glared at her suspiciously and ran away. My mother became tough and very independent early in her life and she wanted me to be strong and independent like she was. That is why she has always encouraged me to be strong and to be optimistic , no matter what. She never tolerated "'sulking" or self-defeating attitudes, so I was able to try to succeed despite all of my own hardships and was able to relate to my mother in many ways. She was my inspiration especially during my years with George. It was reaffirming to see her positive side, after I got involved in therapy - the side that had always been there, but which I never had the desire to focus on before. I now also liked her sense of humor and "fun side". I began to see things in her that I had never seen in the past.

My mother was also "shocked" to hear my complaints about George and his temper. His difficult side made me feel tremendously ashamed but, during that time, I was continually comforted by my blossoming relationship with my mother. However, "What about my father?" I silently wondered about this at the same time. Why did loving one parent have to mean "ditching" the other? *Why were my parents so angry at each other?* I was suddenly tortured by wondering about this. While staying with Dorothy, while I rented her room, in one of the conversations we had before I left, I had been alerted by her when she told me that she felt my parents were making me choose between the two of them. I don't think that either one of them ever intentionally wanted me to do that. I know now that the two of them just had very, very different perspectives about how my symptoms and life challenges should be handled.

I knew now that *I had to see my therapist* at mental health and seek more treatment, even though I didn't feel I deserved any help anymore. Truthfully, I also no longer desired to go to Mental Health at all, but despite all of this, I was wise enough to force myself to continue going. I wasn't even sure anymore if they could get me back on the right track at this point, but I was desperate to get real help now, having extreme feelings of urgency and terror. I felt that I had been truly defeated now and worse, I felt I that I actually really deserved to fail. For the first time, after that incident of not being able to go to work, I now was seriously convinced that I would not be able to take care of myself, as an adult, anymore. My life was now quickly falling apart, so I finally admitted to my psychiatrist and to my tall therapist that nothing we were trying was working. I was still hearing voices, and I still didn't feel confident or functional at all. I couldn't even look directly at my Tall Therapist, as I tried to speak to her. I also had no idea what she was also about to tell me.

She told me they had determined that I definitely had schizophrenia - something I knew nothing about then. My formal diagnosis was Schizoaffective Disorder/Manic Type. My first thought, of course, was that she was blowing things way out of proportion and it would be found out that I didn't really have that disease after all. I was also scared that somebody there had made a big mistake. Ultimately, I did not want to be labeled or considered as someone "mentally" disabled but I had come to the end of my rope. In order to improve my life, I had to accept what they were indicating to me. She also told me that she felt she and the team at Mental Health had no other choice now but to apply for Social Security Disability benefits for me. Despite my desire to be "normal" and "able" this had become a dire need now, and it was their opinion that I desperately needed the benefits which the team at Mental Health immediately qualified me for. This was a big surprise to me because I didn't know that someone with my complaints would qualify as "disabled". At that point, I felt very thankful overall, and definitely breathed a sigh of relief! The "warmth" I initially got from Mental Health at this moment was also very reassuring but I now also felt a new pressure from them to really try to get myself "well".

My renewed faith in psychiatric treatment and the positive experience that getting approved for benefits created for me wasn't, by any means, the end of my problems, as a person, or as a person *with schizophrenia*. I still continued to struggle with some very serious issues at first, although I did, now, have a reliable basic income from social security and a somewhat stable friend in George. I did try hard to remain positive but felt, for the most part, that all of my failed endeavors still were *haunting* me. I realize now that I still desperately needed the right medication, but I didn't know it at the time. My experience with the medications I had tried before, in every attempt, had always seemed to somehow obstruct the normalcy I was trying to achieve. My father's belief that *the psychiatrist's practice in medicating was "tyranny*[41]" was still also weighing so heavily on my mind. Even though my father and I had come close to reuniting at one point, I still remembered how he had warned me, in ominous tones, about seeing a psychiatrist. He would also always warn me that George and my mom were "suppressive" and that was the reason why I was doing so poorly.

I *knew* with my own certainty, that I had to choose to avoid

---

[41] The Scientology Handbook, L. Ron Hubbard

my father now because he would reject George, my mother, my treatment at Mental Health, and myself if I ever did get the chance to see him. I couldn't handle much more negativity in my life and especially any more resistance from my father. I actually had come to *fear him* in a certain regard. Was the real problem that my father was just a kooky alcoholic? *Or maybe ... he was really right*! What was the truth? I was so confused.

I stayed alone - wondering and worrying. My own prolonged feeling of helplessness and total embarrassment brought on by my voices terrorized me all of the time. Survival for me, by this time, also meant making certain that I never would have to experience the "The FACE" falling off my head, so to speak, but at the same time, I could feel it's threat more and more. The more weary and tired I got ,the more I could feel "them" – the voices or "The FACE" - trying to seize me. Despite my terror, I also, secretly, now still wanted to live without having to take any medication at all! Having tried three different medications, and failed at improving from them each time- now was making me feel like a walking hallow chocolate Easter bunny as my problems still multiplied and I was almost *frantic about all of this sometimes*. It felt as if my mind was a real battlefield now.

Since I was no longer working and now constantly feeling socially rejected, I began to have trouble going anywhere, even to the supermarket. It was as if others were always "passing out citations" just by the way they looked at me! My perceptions about others' reactions toward me were most likely completely delusional, but at one point, during an outing with the family I complained to my mother that "others were always giving me dirty looks". Ultimately, because of "The FACE", my biggest fear was the possibility of becoming somebody you would see in a circus. I tried to think positive - that nothing could be *that bad* and I still continued to receive treatment at Mental Health, even though I was secretly irritated and anxious with them. I had now become *afraid* to even return to see them most of the time. This all made me feel terribly scared and incompetent.

I sometimes fell into a "nothingness" in which I would hear my father's voice or my mother raising hers! It *was my fault - I knew now* - because I had schizophrenia and something mysterious was in control of me, although ever so elusively. Then, in 1993, after struggling with all of these thoughts, I finally got completely depressed very suddenly and unexpectedly about my entire life. George seemed to be very distant that day and suddenly walked out of the room to do some wood carving, his "creative" hobby. As my spirits plunged unexpectedly, I thought he was abandoning me, got even more depressed, and decided to take three of my old anti-depressant pills to make myself really, really, sick. I know now that this was really my desperate plea for more attention from him or from someone in my life because I had never seriously thought of suicide before. Yet, I really came close to it that day. I ended up only getting extremely sick and vomiting three times. I lay there on the bathroom floor for a long time, only half dressed because of the heat, and curled up in a fetal position. George never even knew what had happened. He was too busy carving.

I had just become too depressed to ignore the constant threat "The FACE" presented me with, to escape my situation and leave George like I felt my father would have instructed me to do. I could no longer even make decisions for myself and felt literally helpless. I still desperately tried to feel happy but my quality of life seemed so hopeless, too. Above all, I felt by being on disability and no longer working, I had completely lost my dignity. I also suspected that Mental Health felt really sorry for me and secretly hated that I might actually be earning their pity. After all, in addition to receiving more social services I had also recently sold my soul for a roof over my head – and I had done so to a first unassuming, but now surprisingly cheerful older man named George - and he didn't even have a clue.

I also had sacrificed my relationship with my father and was now faced with the realization that there was no hope for our once wonderful father-daughter relationship anymore. The absence of my father hurt me unbearably. He couldn't save me

111

anymore, like he always had done, when I reached out to him in the past because – on a certain level - I had chosen mental health, instead of him. And, making matters even worse - my tall beautiful therapist would soon transfer to another clinic, while another therapist replaced her who was a lot less compassionate. I desperately wanted to escape my guilty, confused, frantic existence because now it was really killing me inside! Most significant to me was my still lingering belief – that Mental Health still had no idea about what I was constantly running from ...

I was so secretive about "The FACE", but looking back now, it was really the only true, persistent, and major reason I was going through all of these failures and eventually refusing every medication they tried. The FACE" was the seemingly overpowering force that had first put me in this awful predicament - and it was still keeping me there ...

At the end of 1993, it seemed as though I had finally and dangerously gone too far. I was 26 by this time and, although I had not, at first, realized how serious it really was, I was now hopelessly immersed into a growing inner world - and falling into something that *really could have ended in disaster.*

Amidst the Dream (1989)

... "Wild Horses" perpetually surrounding me -
dreams in motion, all around me - boldly
running away with my psyche. ... (pg, 98)

Into the Light (2015)

"This new beginning would mean a new life for me without as many disturbing anxieties... I was now so much more comfortable in my own skin which allowed me to feel more like other people ..

CHAPTER SEVEN

Escaping The Storms

My psychiatrist now seemed to know about my persistent delusions and demons, although I had been careful not to tell *anyone* at all about many of the thoughts that were constantly circulating in my mind. I was now living in a waking nightmare and he knew by now that something was really desperately wrong with me. On one particular visit, avoiding eye contact with him, I finally admitted with hopeless terror that I was starting to think that I couldn't work at all anymore and shared everything I had been trying to hide from him. He responded simply by saying, "Don't lose any sleep over it". His words seemed very odd to me at first, but I realize now that his somewhat "casual" optimism was based on experience. He was about to provide the perfect solution for me – and I was also now ready to try to trust him and really listen. He insisted that I *must* agree to try a very high potency antipsychotic drug called Haldol – by injection.

He stated that these powerful injections were my last and only alternative because I had not been reliably conforming to any of the prescribed drug treatment plans suggested in the past, in particular the antipsychotic medication. Before this, my own pattern, as I have explained, was to perhaps try something for a few days, then decide on my own that I didn't need it, and then report to him that it didn't work. My psychiatrist also warned me that this monthly supervised injection was really a true last ditch effort, since I had been resisting anything or everything else. The injections would assure him I was taking the medication he knew I needed so badly, regularly and faithfully. He had finally become really frustrated with me, and in his words, would no longer risk me becoming a "walking medicine cabinet". I felt now as if I would do anything to convince him that I was willing to try. Although still feeling very doubtful this newest idea would work, I agreed to comply.

Haldol is a commonly used anti-psychotic drug, tried and true, but very powerful. It is not only used to treat schizophrenia and psychosis, it is also sometimes used to treat anger. Under injection therapy, I would go to mental health every month to get one long-acting shot that would last an entire 30 days. Surprising results occurred for me, almost immediately. The Haldol worked very well, making some of my delusions, voices and "demons" recede from the forefront of my mind and, especially important for me, become less intimidating. It was an "instant miracle" in my case, although I have learned that medication does not always work as quickly. This new beginning would mean a new life for me without as many disturbing anxieties and debilitating feelings of anger, along with the helplessness that my anger had been causing! I was now so much more comfortable in my own skin which allowed me to feel more like other people. Amazingly, the pain and anxiety I had been experiencing also seemed to have completely subsided.

Haldol would be the first high potency drug I had ever agreed to take regularly and I think that my psychiatrist may have been just as pleased as I was with the results. He now seemed to be a lot more willing to listen to my problems and sometimes even more sympathetic and understanding. I also finally felt a very "welcoming" feeling from the entire Mental Health team as well. After all those years of emotional hardship, struggles, failed relationships and the loss of friends and my family's faith in me, suddenly I had my very own answer. Now, after struggling for so long to do it on my own, or to handle my symptoms using Scientology, positive thinking, "mind over matter" or a host of other solutions, I realized that this medication – just one injection once a month was exactly what I needed. I had finally been successful in finding and – even more importantly - agreeing with - an effective, and successful drug and therapeutic regiment!

My psychiatrist who brought out the "well" side of me, still caused me a little anxiety, despite all of the approval I was now receiving from others. I secretly knew that, despite my obvious improvement, I *really wasn't entirely "well"* as far as my inner dialect was concerned during the beginning stages of my Haldol treatment and that my broadcasting was *still* delusional. Thankfully, though, my own inner dialect and broadcasting was still not as *bad* as it had been before. I also began to wonder if, since they had already declared me disabled, Mental Health would now expect me to seek work. Since I had already tried so hard and lost so many jobs, that workplace insecurity also caused me quite a bit of anxiety throughout my new treatment. Now, I still really didn't know *who I was anymore* or if I was even being accepted within *my own* reality. And - for *the first time* - because the Haldol was now working so well, I began to understand that *maybe I actually really did have the disease of schizophrenia.* I finally began to try to accept that this could really be true, after all.

I would also learn later that Haldol, although it is a strong antipsychotic drug, does NOT take away all of "the voices" completely or forever. The big, wonderful difference, however, was that I became able to exist a lot better. I could now live - both *with* and *despite* - my voices. Most significantly, it really helped me with my fears, anxieties and anger as I slowly started to improve in many, many ways. I could now enjoy time with others and also my own time, alone, with myself. Haldol also gave me much more control over sorting out what was real *and* what was not real. I no longer reflected upon my days with 'Sweetheart" Red, or Russell anymore for my own sanity. Whatever behaviors I had at that time had ended. *I now got the sense that all of my behaviors had been forced in the past because they never had actually felt natural to me.* I began to feel my past efforts to relate had been nothing but an act. Now that those were not continually being reinforced, they never returned.

Since the Haldol worked so well with *anger* I was also now

able to understand myself better. I had always, outwardly, been very passive, but a persistent wave of rage had almost always been present inside me without my full knowledge because I had tried so hard but seemingly - *always* had failed! Now, I was breathing a lot slower and not as panicky as before. I had finally found George, who seemed somewhat comfortable to be around, but I often thought at times, that maybe George wasn't ideal for me, either, and that I shouldn't be letting George turn me into what I still thought was *such a mess*, especially after that fateful day that he shouted at me. I could easily forgive George for the shouting incident in my heart but not entirely in my mind. He seemed to accept me, but it was not easy to ignore that powerful spirited facet of my soul - a part that was sacred and still belonged, in many ways, to my father. This was now *the past.*

I soon began to feel that my true identity was not to be a successful, independent, young woman, after all and then I suddenly felt that I was to meant to care for George. I was alone at the house while George worked part-time during the day and, even though my medication helped, it was still sometimes difficult for me while he was gone. My role was to clean house, grocery shop and cook. When George came home in the evenings he had the brightest smile which, coincidently, was sort of like my mother's smile. I was always in heaven during those moments and so happy to have the house clean and dinner ready for him! He knew I loved him and I loved his handsome face! I also spent a lot of time watching TV with George in the evenings at first.

One evening while George and I were watching television something magical happened. A baby cried. It was a significant change for me, that the sound was no longer painful for me to hear. It was a completely new experience and a true "medication miracle"!

I was also fortunate that George had no problem with me

118

staying in touch with my family. My mother and my sister were both happy to have "me back" and noticed the difference in me almost right away. My mother was more confident that she now had her *"real daughter"* again. Our family get-togethers were mainly on holidays and now I could actually engage in conversations with my relatives! These interactions were all very exciting and new for me, but sometimes I would still find myself getting extremely uncomfortable. I would begin to fear at times that, even though I was now more communicative because of the medication, I still might, all of a sudden, reveal the troubled, hidden side of myself.

I questioned everything during family interactions now - myself - as well as my family members. It was difficult for me to comprehend where the emotional pull of gravity always seemed to take me. It also became apparent to me that I couldn't please too many people all at once. For instance, interacting with one family member could get interrupted by another person's facial expression or comment. It was often stressful and unpleasant for me. Thinking back, since I was beginning to find solace in art more now, it could have been the restless artist in me who didn't want to be in one place or social situation for too long. It also could have been another reflection of my shattered existence.

I took Haldol for a total of seven years. That was a very long time period when, in order to attempt to get better, I was forced to also cope with Haldol's grueling side effects.[42] In fact, it is a drug known for some of the worst side effects of them all and I quickly learned that, at any time, I could become Haldol's *victim*! I would suffer from unexpected stiffening in my body and involuntarily movements. At times, I also experienced uncontrollable trembling and this created episodes for me that were almost equivalent to seizures. When I felt the side effects coming on, I would have to spend time in my room, alone,

---

[42] Patients on Haldol may respond to stress very poorly, and stress produces these side effects. Torrey 2001

separated from George, and would just lay in my bed overwhelmed by a deluge of horrible sensations. I would sometimes hear scary voices coming from people I knew or used to know! They were always very mean voices that fought me, intimidated me, and challenged me. I often begged for them to just please go away. When they became forefront, I felt for certain that anyone I had attacked with my internal broadcasting was now getting even with me. It was horrifying and it felt so real, not as if I were imagining it all - like it was really happening!

The most shocking of those incidents was when I saw my male psychiatrist standing in my room by my bed during one episode! I later tried to analyze that nightmare vision and didn't understand why it scared me so bad. Yet, despite those horrors, I was grateful for my Haldol, overall, and would not give up on it. I was somewhat overwhelmed with the side effects, but I comforted myself with the thought that I usually only got them once a month or less. I was also able, due to my medication, to realize that the negative experiences were "side effects" and not completely real, although they often seemed to be. I came to expect, but also to accept them more as time went on and to accept the good, along with the bad.

I was also certain that George, who overall, gave me a lot of support and allowed me to improve while on Haldol, truly needed me. I wanted to somehow further harness my old comfortable childhood moments as well, so I stayed with the Haldol and George for many years to come very faithfully. I also came to realize that Haldol wasn't going to solve everything for me right away. I still had a problem with being alone and with the frightening voices during certain times, even while faithfully taking my medication. I also continued to have no social life of my own to feel part of or to relish in as I had somewhat peacefully done at times in the past. I did not want to go to group outings with other "mentally disabled persons" or any activities like that in which my therapist had offered. I still wanted to maintain a certain thread of "normalcy" and of my own independence.

Instead of seeking a "social life" now, I would analyze my "voices" when not doing art. Being alone in the house seemed to create a lot of unused fearful energy in me despite the Haldol. I still wasn't sorting and discarding experiences like most other people do. I couldn't focus on reading and I also couldn't focus on television, although it's background noise or that of a children's show sometimes comforted me a little. All I could think of at times was my painful past, even more than I ever did before. I also continued to retreat into my inner world fantasies during my first year on Haldol, still imagining that I had the power to shape my world with those thoughts. I concluded that Haldol had at least given me the chance to soften and nearly eliminate the power of the formerly persistent "broadcasting voices" I had formerly been helpless against. Now I believed that I could alleviate any further inner turmoil with my inner world fantasies. Even at my best, I still couldn't completely relate to a seemingly very distant mental health staff despite the fact that I now wanted their approval.

"I shouldn't continue this angry internal broadcasting anymore," I often told myself. I felt frustrated about it - but I still continued to do it.

I also kept my broadcasting behavior, as well as other secrets, from both my therapist and psychiatrist for a total of six years. I had made a promise to myself that I would keep some things secret to avoid being pressured into taking higher doses of medication or combinations of medications and risk becoming a "zombie" (this reflected both my dad's and my own fear about taking medication). I still believed, deep down, that I could just handle my inner world with my own mind somehow, someday, but I also knew that these persistent variations of broadcasting behavior could not keep continuing! I knew that, so I was afraid of what might happen. At the same time, I also remained afraid to tell anyone at Mental Health about this for fear that *maybe they had heard some of my voices.* It all often

121

felt so real, and my thinking about it became like an obsession. I had times where I could *not* get a thought out of my head. It was almost constant and it replaced normal concentration. As my obsessive thoughts were forefront, I felt feelings of guilt and shame time and time again. I even secretly believed that maybe I had caused the grunge movement and killed millions of people with my broadcasting. I didn't realize then that the broadcasting I had experienced so as well as my way of ridding myself of obsessive thoughts through fantasies are classified as simply symptoms of my disease, along with "delusions of grandeur." Over time, I have also come to personally believe that these symptoms are related to General Anxiety Disorder as well.[43]

During my early treatment, I faced another challenge. I had to try really hard to accept the brutal reality that Haldol *had changed the way I looked!* My face now looked really different to me, so I stared at myself in the mirror every day. When I started to hear voices, I would often glance at myself in the mirror and I would not seem as attractive when I looked at myself. Now that I look back, I believe that, along with the actual facial changes that Haldol *does* often cause, I may have also been suffering like those who suffer from *a form of Body Dysmorphic Disorder* at that time[44]. I tried really hard not to think about the changes in my appearance too much. At least "The FACE", the twisting ugly demon from my past, was now for the most part, a raging storm of the past! I had actually escaped and conquered the never-ending obstacles and terrors I had suffered from "The FACE" now and could give all of the credit – totally - to Haldol for this. Overall, I was very grateful.

As I became more familiar with Haldol I could then became occupied with trying to feel more comfortable in my own skin. I tried to do this in any way I could and on some rare occasions it was nice to just be able to do exactly what I felt like doing. I

---

[43] See Chapter 3

[44] Body Dysmorphic Disorder is an obsessive preoccupation with some aspect of one's appearance. (British Medical Journal 2004)

could actually begin to remember again how it was before my illness ever started and to sometimes concentrate on something that interested me. When I was able to do this, it would naturally eliminate my "broadcasting". I still sometimes dreamed about Adonis, but now that I was on Haldol, I also realized, deep down, that he was, obviously, unattainable for me. I also secretly felt that I could be doing a lot better with a more suitable social network, but learned to accept my social status overall. Thankfully, I was no longer having to try to be to be enthusiastic and unattainably high functioning for the sake of my peers, but I missed that, too, in a certain regard.

Most important, I was feeling much more relaxed and would go on eventually to develop a new sense of self. The time eventually came to start my own "recovery program". I actually attended classes part-time at Oxnard City College again! This was very special to me because I could finally finish what I had started when I was dating Russell. I discouraged myself from having as many delusions with encouragement from my mother to keep remaining positive. I eventually received my Associates Degree in General Liberal Arts and Sciences. I also did a lot of painting in George's third bedroom and participated in an Art Therapy Program at the historic Camarillo State Hospital.[45] with my mother. She would drive us through the beautiful strawberry fields and up the quiet, winding road to the hospital and since there was hardly any traffic it seemed like a peaceful retreat. There were many other mentally ill and developmentally disabled people from all walks of life at the hospital, some extremely debilitated and others a lot like myself and I began to feel very grateful.

Jack Cheney and Leslie Hara, supervisors of the "Art is Life" program there were "bohemian", very spiritually positive types so I also always felt accepted. Their purpose was to create art with the mentally ill in a relaxed therapeutic atmosphere and

---

[45] One of the few remaining "mental hospitals" in California, Camarillo State Hospital was later transformed into California State University Channel Islands

then display the clients' work at two big weekend Art Shows each year a for the general public to purchase. My mother and I both sold our original paintings and drawings there, which was very beneficial and healthy for both of us. After these fun and relaxing outings   it was almost impossible for me to just sit in front of the television most of the time, anymore. I made it a top priority to get out in the world more.

Shortly after my positive experience with the art therapy program, I had another very positive experience when I received a long awaited surprise! A lady who lived near my mother and who rescued cats had a beautiful baby calico cat that she was trying to find a home for. I immediately wanted her, got her, and named my new family member "Candy Cat". She was now the "quiet and functioning" part of my mind and I would become very protective of her. I was told by the lady who gave her to me that she survived jumping from a very large building unscathed! She was a quirky and talkative cat who always followed me around the house. My Candy Cat would soon become more important to me than anything else in my world.

Over time, after going back to school, participating in the art program and adopting my Candy Cat - despite my delusions - I was feeling more hopeful than I ever had before. Haldol had successfully reduced the impact of intrusive thoughts and delusions on my thinking and behavior, so I actually finally felt more normal. I wanted to see my father now but, at the same time, I was also *terrified at just the thought of seeing him*. So much had changed about me by this time and my conflicted past with my father was now becoming an uncomfortable memory. It hurt constantly to think about our now ultimately non-existent relationship and to know that he wasn't with me on my new journey. Worse still, now that I was working compliantly with a therapist and psychiatrist and taking medication, I knew for certain that I would be considered "dangerous" by him and other Scientologists, according to Church of Scientology teachings. My father had taught me that Scientologists do not want to be around anyone on psychotropic drugs, not even their own family members. That caution also extended to most other forms of medication, too (my father even hesitated to take aspirin for a headache). After battling against taking medication for so long, and trying to remain loyal to my father, facing him as the newly "labeled" schizophrenic on potent psychotropic medication would be very hard for me to do.

I just kept putting off seeing him. This whole new "reality" between us was very hard for me to face. I had always respected Scientology as a young person and still do in many ways. However, now, my former tendency to blame others and label them as "suppressive" (a Scientology term) seemed way too harsh to me. All of my life, up until being medicated, I had felt it was okay to evaluate every little thing about a person, such as their emotional makeup, in order to determine when and if to avoid them. Now I was questioning that and feeling very guilty about those teachings and my old coping mechanisms, but it was also very hard for me to break the cycle.

Sadly, in 1997, although my father was somewhat successful, independent, and very tough in his own way, he hit "rock bottom" with alcoholism. He was a brilliant man, but with such a serious problem, I had already imagined he would probably end up desperate someday. Now, he really needed help with his basic survival needs from George and I so, despite my own fears and recent attempts to avoid an inevitable conflict with my father, it was time to go see him. George and I made plans to drive to Los Angeles for a visit, pick up some of his artwork and to help him out financially. On the way there, I was still a little bit hopeful about seeing my father again, despite the fact that during our earlier phone conversation, his tone had been cautionary. It was a *warning* tone which I had never heard in his voice while speaking with me before.

When we did arrive and meet with him, the tension in the air was unbearable. George was terrifyingly quiet the whole time and seemed almost threatened by my father's presence. It seemed as if he did not like my father and my father was more tense than I had ever seen him. It did not surprise me that much, because George was a recovering alcoholic and my dad was still drinking! I was so conflicted between my love for both of them that I couldn't take a side. I wanted to, but it seemed that I just couldn't win. Despite this, I was very happy to be by my father's side again.

George still had enough heart to help my father out financially. George always *did always have a big heart* underneath it all! My father, the reason for most of my confidence all of my life, surprisingly really didn't seem to express anything good or bad about George or about anything else that day! I do, thankfully, still remember that meeting and it was special to me despite some of the tension. It would be one of our very last meetings when my father was still "himself". His own mental health would change drastically in the near future. That day in Los Angeles I was still "his girl" like always.

My father and I would never talk about those challenging moments or feelings that day at all. I just remember that his presence in my life on that day had really changed me for the better once again. That was my father, and who he was. He always saved me in the worst of circumstances. Overall, it gave me more normalcy than I ever felt to see him again and I had also avoided the conflict about medication that I had feared that day... I still had George for the support that I needed too, which was finally an affirmation.

At the end of 1997, I was feeling even more strong-willed, determined, and experiencing really positive approval from mental health, as well as from my father and mother. So, I decided to venture even further and get a job through the Department of Rehabilitation. I was successful and soon obtained regular employment at a key shop in the neighboring city of Ventura. My new job making keys at a charming little kiosk was a great success! It was a wonderful job and I loved working there! My job required that I develop the skill of making keys, a gratifying feeling of accomplishment for me because I learned to do it well and I was so proud of my work! Even the somewhat long drive from Oxnard to work was, itself, also very liberating - and well worth it.

At first, I was still cautious about the public, I had to imagine and remind myself constantly, that the customers were actually really "angels" coming to see me at my little job kiosk. Thinking that way was my "lifeline" for the entire first year that I worked there. I had to take "baby steps" about my thinking process and how I looked at life and other people. Then, over time, with some more positive self-talk, I was slowly able to create even more positive, affirming thoughts and some "inner talk" that was healthy for me . Gradually, this new chapter in my life made me feel unaffected about so many things that had once bothered me. I also was fortunate to have a "job coach" through the Department of Rehabilitation who was very effective in helping me. As a former therapist, he was a great listener and he even would sit alongside me in the kiosk for about six months to give me the support I needed.

I did worry while I was at work, at first, about my home life. I was afraid that George would harm me because of my new independence and I had a scary nightmare one night about him holding a knife after I first started my job. Thankfully, that never happened and living with George, while working, became a little more peaceful after a while. He did have issues with women and "out of the blue", shortly after I began my job, he once opened up to me about *his problems with how he treated women*. I was a little surprised at his shocking confession, even though he didn't reveal much in detail. I had come to expect only a "strong, silent" demeanor from George. I always suspected that he could be capable of violence with me, right from the start, but he would only shout at me and push me one time during what would eventually become our eleven years together. George even eventually started to call me at work a lot with a "cheerful" tone in his voice and he wrote me a beautiful birthday card once. Those gestures from him were the biggest shock of my life!

My boss was also very supportive during my time at the kiosk and I thought about her a lot. Her voice comforted me more than anything else did and I really looked up to her. She also seemed to like me a lot and value both me and my work there. She was a somewhat friendly and headstrong woman who confided in me, surprisingly, like a real friend. I always felt very grateful that she was my boss the entire time I worked there. With her support and encouragement, I would continue to practice and improve my comfort level with customers at the shop too. I also felt very proud to have developed the real skill of making keys that worked well and it didn't matter as much to me anymore how my customers judged me. I was now a skilled craftsperson. People didn't come to see me, or the boss, for that matter. They came because we made the best keys in town! That was our reputation at the key shop and we were complimented about that constantly.

It was a very for happy time for us. Since I had, by this time, also learned from therapy that anger was okay, I even stuck up for myself a couple of times with a customer and nothing horrible happened. I also practiced, while I was at the key shop, trying not to internally broadcast as much anymore with what I perceived to be my "super-human mind powers" like my delusions had caused me to do in the past. Since I had experienced trouble processing thoughts in my past without broadcasting, my obsessive thoughts would sometimes intrude upon me but I learned to handle it well. Since I now had more of an income, it was also relaxing for me to go shopping sometimes or to pay a little more attention to a book or to a creative project. Even though I was on a strict schedule of antipsychotic medication at that time, I would find out later in life, that I was *not being treated then* for my frequent, ongoing, obsessive thoughts. This would not be recognized and treated until much later (in 2012) by my third psychiatrist. So, I was still continuing, earlier, to live with not only the anxiety these thoughts caused, but with shame about this behavioral symptom as well. On my bad days, I often had to remind myself that my "evil spirits" and my obsessions did not have as much of an "infectious" power as I sometimes thought they did.

Thankfully, my psychiatrist finally switched me to the

128

newer, modern version of Haldol, a medication called Zyprexa in 2001. I complied with my treatment fully and was thankful to find out that my trembling episodes finally stopped![46] Zyprexa also made me feel much more normal and let me express myself more fully as an artist. At the same time, it enabled me to appreciate life and a new improved physical well-being, so it was a much better medication experience for me. I still battled with my spiritual beliefs and I had read that the ideal path for me was to go ahead and let myself have my fantasies occasionally while sticking with my medication, so that's what I did. My life became much easier and I would sometimes even just leave the house on a whim to go shopping! Zyprexa did have a somewhat sedating effect like Haldol, so to counteract this, I would drink caffeinated soda drinks and I also smoked cigarettes occasionally. It took years but, eventually, I became a little more careful about what I put into my body because Zyprexa (even though a newer drug) can sometimes cause obesity as well.

In Spring of 2001 my City College loan was finally paid in full. I took my mother's advice and eagerly returned to school at the new California State University Channel Islands. It is located where the old Camarillo State Hospital once stood. With the help of financial aid, I was able to attend classes half-time and I majored in General Liberal Arts and Sciences for a total of two semesters. I was really hoping to find out if I would actually be capable of getting a Bachelor's Degree. The campus was very spacious, the professors were welcoming and overall, it was very exciting to feel I was a part of something that was, in a sense, bigger than myself. Significantly, I experienced no symptoms of schizophrenia while I was on-campus attending the university and for me that was another "medication miracle". Thinking back, it definitely didn't feel the same, all alone, on my new university campus as it had felt on my old high school campus, making the high school float, having a

---

[46] Please see Chapter Notes about the medication Zyprexa

handsome boyfriend that loved me and I was proud of. It was different, but similar somehow. At least now, while attending college again, I was having some positive thoughts on campus and at home at times. This may also have been due to the totally new relationship with my mother that was evolving at the time.

I stayed with George for eleven years, and I have always been grateful for that time period – especially for *him and* for my very successful job at the key shop. When I finally lost George to pancreatic cancer in 2003, it was for me, as you might imagine, a very devastating loss. He was only 58 years of age, but the doctors told me it was a miracle that he lived as long as he did with his weight problem. I took especially good care of him as his illness progressed, as I always had, cooking him nutritious food and making protein shakes for him. I tried so hard to do anything and everything I could to help him. He battled his illness like a champion, even maintaining his great sense of humor almost until the end. George had a wonderful talent with comedy and was constantly creating really funny jokes. As a professional comedian, he probably could have been a big gift to this world. [47] His sense of humor was another good quality that made my own life more bearable with him no matter what mood I was in. He could almost always make others laugh, even my mother, and she is a pretty serious person. I wish I could have seen him do this for many more years.

I think that George was just troubled, though, as most misplaced artists and entertainers are, because of his "greatness". I had always appreciated his creative side and his many wood carving hobby projects. George was really brilliant underneath it all. He was always so full of life and had so many friends who called him to hear a joke or two. He always stayed strong throughout everything and this was a trait that I pray maybe I have gained from my many years of being with him.

---

[47] "Top scale artists are the most powerful people on earth for aesthetics is the quickest method for lifting large numbers of people up-tone." (Minshull, Hubbard 1972)

Near the end I would often lay close to him and in the final days before he left the world, he told me he would be "watching over me". I knew the minute a cab driver came to take him away from our home that he wouldn't be coming back. I visited him that same night at the hospital and on the next day. My treasured, and literally life-saving relationship with my very faithful, familiar friend was near an end. He was about to leave this world from a hospital bed - never to return! It was unbelievable that this could be happening - I still wanted to tell him so many things.

He told me not to cry but, instead, to hold my head up high, as I tried to touch his cheek when I visited him. I turned away, feeling like that hollow Easter bunny again, as I left his room. Sadly, I was not there when he passed away. I had been waiting to get my strength back in order to go back. The word that he passed on his second day at the hospital, came to me from a nurse who admired him there. I made arrangements for his ashes and contacted his family members. I had been given the responsibility of trying to make sure each one got the belongings of his that they wanted to have after he passed away. My little sister stayed with me at my home the evening after he passed, as well as for a while afterward, thankfully. She gave me the moral support I really needed at that time.

Now, completely on my own again, in September, 2003 - I was very alone again. I had to force myself to somehow survive and to somehow be optimistic. There was a lot for me to do in order to make it on my own without George. I had decided to try and find a roommate so I could stay in the house we had shared. At the same time, I was hoping that the Section 8 housing, George and I had applied for together in 2001, would somehow come through soon because I was still not comfortable about living in that big house alone or in sharing it with complete strangers. Added to that, my professional life working at the key shop would became somewhat unstable, and I soon realized, even more, how much George had meant to me. My boss and I began, unexpectedly, to have some communication problems and, unfortunately, my job coach was no longer there to help. I was feeling new pressures during this very difficult time period but I tried to keep working as my delusional mind and old coping mechanisms suddenly advanced to the "forefront" again. I would continue to work at the key shop for several more years but it never was the same anymore.

Thankfully, and miraculously, Section 8 housing did come through for me only two months after George passed away. It seemed almost heaven sent, especially since the waiting lists were so long. I felt so relieved and so excited once again, but also very scared – and all at the same time. I could now, at least hopefully, find a small apartment and begin to live independently on my own. I had already experienced my share of roommate challenges and problems since I left home. I had already lived with a total of three men, the Amway couple, two women, Dorothy and Adelle. All of these living situations were often questionable and sometimes uncomfortable or even unbearable. Housing assistance was now, obviously, a dream come true for me! My mother was also very happy and relieved for me that I would not have to struggle with alternative living arrangements anymore. My schizophrenic grandmother, who I would have loved to have met, had ended up homeless with her belongings in a shopping cart, the last time my mother saw her. My mother had always feared that either she, herself - or I (after I started showing symptoms of illness) would become that same "lost" homeless lady someday.

The tragedies were not yet over for me and for those I loved so much, though. My father, by this time, had moved to Hawaii and only written me once. The next word I got about him was from a social worker at a hospital, informing me that he had suffered a heart attack and now had dementia. He had been facing his own problems with jobs when he arrived there and had been staying in a homeless shelter. I was appointed to be his legal guardian and he was transported from Hawaii to California to live in a nursing home near me in Port Hueneme. It was a big responsibility for me to take on, but I loved my father and did everything I could for him. Sadly, he ended up in his final years as a man that "I no longer knew." Ironically, he now even suffered from frequent delusions, himself. One afternoon when my mother and I took him out to lunch, he even talked to his deceased sister on an imaginary phone he thought he was holding in his hands.

Because of his serious dementia, my father was forced to be on potent psychiatric medication, probably stronger than mine, in order to control his behavior and impulses. This all seemed so tragic for him, a man who, as a Scientologist, did not believe in pharmaceutical drugs. He must have hated taking them and being restrained there. He even tried to jump over the fence of his nursing home on four or five occasions! I would repeatedly have to pick him up from the emergency hospital with gashes on his head that required stitches. At those times, he would always cry out to me "I just want to be free!" when I arrived to pick him up and return him to the nursing home. I think that he maintained the belief that I should be taking care of him, or that he should be living with me and not in the home, but that was completely impossible. He was really just too ill to function without being restrained and supervised by professionals continually. It was so tragic an ending and my heart fell apart every time I even thought about him.

My father was still a fighter/survivor through all of this and managed to live for nine more years in this horrible condition. There was no other solution for him, because he had lost his entire grip on reality and could not care for himself. He would become a lot more frustrated, even bitter about his own limitations and living condition, as time went on, and would sometimes lash out at me. I still had to somehow make the extra effort to show him I cared and it was sometimes extremely difficult. In 2007, when he died at the Shoreline nursing home at the age of 69, I visited him briefly to say goodbye. I am certain his last decade had been a living nightmare for him. He was too brilliant of a person to end up that way.

I always understood my father and I truly understood even

133

more about him, when a friend of his brought me some of his belongings. There were several old photos, his writings, some art work and some Scientology material that his friends had kept safe for him. My Dad was actually very handsome as a young man and in one photo I found, he reminded me of myself before my illness and diagnosis. I was really glad to have some of his belongings for myself, but after seeing them, I was even more tortured to think of his final years, having lost all of his freedom in that nursing home.

It was very painful at first but the "God" who my father believed in and taught me to believe in had called him away for a reason. I told myself that when I would feel the pain. It began to seem that "God " was watching over me - and that my own higher power would soon return with an abundance of mercy and unlimited blessings for me and for my future dreams.

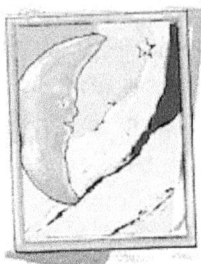

Cosmic Sky (2012)

Thank you Dad, most of all for
coming back to me.
It was through President
Obama that I saw you
once again.
I saw you in your jacket
(my favorite)
It was Obama's jacket
reminding me.
I felt your warmth
although you were not there.

134

Home

We all should
have a home.
Justification for
homelessness is
not a truth.
Someday I know
we will all see
the light that
 burns...

Spiritual Awareness (2005)

Hope Beyond Barriers (2016)

... I feel I have definitely overcome some of the barriers of my illness. Now I can stop that disturbing inner voice and the overwhelming flood of emotions that happened ... I can often feel a natural range of emotions, all at once, and actually control them!

CHAPTER EIGHT

Staying Well

I found a nice apartment for me and my Calico Cat Candy. Now, years later, Candy is no longer with me, but I have two other wonderful cats to share my life with. I also help care for my neighbor's two cats, whom I think of as, and often call "my own". Section 8 housing really helped me and I also believe that George is definitely still watching over me, every day just as he promised he would always do. Because of his example of strength, despite all odds, I have felt responsible enough to live on my own, handle my limited budget and make things work in my life. I had to quit the job at the key shop in 2008. My boss and I had grown apart from each other and I was no longer in a world where my boss was "everything" to me. I couldn't accept our new reality and had been obsessing about her and shopping way too much in an attempt to feel better during the final months I enjoyed working there. The poor economy and George W. Bush were also contributing factors, but I stuck with my job there for a long time, even after I moved into to my own apartment. I stuck with the key shop and with my boss for a total of eleven years - for as long as I possibly could.

My life is totally different now, after years of the appropriate treatment, and in a better way. I try very hard to stay healthy and to do everything possible to counteract any possible negative physical effects related to my medication. I also joined a gym for a while in order to improve my fitness and strength and I try now to exercise as often as I can. I have basically maintained a positive attitude about my condition throughout every challenge I have faced. My troubled past is over now and I realize that I may have, much of the time, in fact, been accepted by other people at my workplace or in other social situations. Yet, because of my mental disorder, my mind was always explaining things differently to me.

This was, then - and still is, now - due to my schizophrenic symptoms and specifically to *how I perceive things*, as I have explained earlier. The outcome of these perceptions, in my earlier years, was speechlessness and a feeling of exclusion and degradation. During High School and College, those negative inner voices and even my better "magical voices" were definitely in command of my life at that time - *instead of me*. I still suffer from that tendency on my bad days but, now - I have *much more* control over them.

Suddenly, I am now in a place where I can also take care of myself while living alone. I no longer live in a big three bedroom house with a man, as I did with George. I live independently now in an apartment with my beloved cats. I do live in a somewhat large apartment complex, among other tenants, though, and I have slowly come to realize that I actually can function in various social relationships. I even find a way, sometimes, to stand up for myself to many types of people. It is not always easy for me but I stayed committed to ongoing therapy with my counselor at Mental Health, faithfully trying to develop better communication and "self-talk" skills and to became more communicative with others. I did improve, after a while, but it took some time. Now it's not so much about convincing someone else that I am okay. It is all about feeling and expressing true feelings in a genuine way and not worrying if my face starts to look a little funny sometimes. Many people around me now know about my condition and I have overcome the negative behavior of "snubbing" someone, most of the time, along with some of my other helpless dysfunctions of the past.

My old inner demon, "The FACE" has actually "saved" me, now and then, because it alerts me when I am not in the right frame of mind. When I accidently do grimace I don't feel like it is the end of the world anymore. It only happens, now, on rare occasions, since I have been on medication. My doctor calls it a "tick". Medication and treatment remain a consistent part of my life and I feel I have accomplished more at this point than I thought I ever would have. I often miss my long-term job success at the key shop, but I still stay busy and very positive.

Today, I am much happier. I now have a new passion - creating and illustrating fun, imaginative, stories for children and I also continue to paint. The computer has become my new best friend and I feel that my writing and illustrating are just as - or even more meaningful than any customer service job like the key shop could be. I now have more control over my own life and have focused on my own self–improvement, luckily, without the "older" medication Haldol of my past. Although I desperately needed it to harness my symptoms, at first, the Zyprexa now works much better for me. Fear and anxiety at times have still caused me some problems like walking in a parking lot or driving but I have successfully maintained a healthy state of mind overall. Sometimes a valuable sentiment or scene will come to my mind as a "voice", as well, and it will make me feel inspired to do a drawing, or a painting or even to write a story. People now say I have a talent for writing, as well as art .

I am very grateful for my new life. I also have a special relationship with my neighbor. Handsome as ever, and very close with his sister, he has always been there by my side for moral support. I relate to both him and his sister in many wonderful ways. I still remain, however, very careful, now, not to ever think of my neighbor, now the love of my life, along with his wonderful cats, as the total solution for my battle against schizophrenia. Now that I am in a much more comfortable place, I can set better boundaries for myself in relationships. So, in essence, I appreciate him, but I try to avoid being too dependent or anxious about him and what he does or says.

I feel I have definitely overcome some of the barriers of my illness.   Now I can stop that disturbing inner voice and the overwhelming flood of emotions that happened mostly around women and that which made me act so inconsiderate. I can often feel a natural range of emotions, all at once, and actually control them! Since I have had my own apartment I have also found

139

that a new positive identity is slowly forming within me. This is, happily, the first time in my life, that I have enjoyed my space just as much as my time spent with my boyfriend. I have even made a few other friends, including some women friends at my apartment complex and that is a very positive accomplishment for me.

It is now as if I was and still am able to start my entire life all over again because I took my antipsychotic medication faithfully and had actually taken the time to read about and accept my condition in 1998. I finally have taken all of the right steps and I am gaining real control of my symptoms. I still often struggle to deal with some very real fears because of this crippling disease, but at least, I have developed some real coping mechanisms. I also try to learn more about and remain updated about my illness, regularly, in order to help both myself and other people. That is part of why I am writing this book.

I also faithfully still visit a psychiatrist in order to treat my illness and I try to comply with his or her suggestions. I try hard to respect what the professionals have to say, even if it sometimes takes me a few days to think things over. This is especially so, when it is suggested that I try something new. When I first began treatment years ago, in the back of my mind, I would always think that, *if I could just try harder* and take the first step by leaving George, my symptoms would stop. Now I realize that this was always impossible, no matter who I was with, without medication and professional help. I also know now that it is always all about helping others and that *what you do comes back to you in this life!* Earlier in my story, I devoted a lot of time and love to helping out and nurturing both my father and George as much as I possibly could during the periods before they passed away. When Section 8 came through for me, somehow, my own needs started suddenly to be met. I still believe in family and helping family and try to help my mother as much as I can.

Looking back now, what I *really needed* is what I have now - a space to myself where I can walk to a kitchen or bathroom without worrying about others confronting me or rearranging my state of mind. I am even content, now, with just being alone sometimes. Difficulties and strange experiences can find their way into everyone's lives and I've had my own share of both. I don't feel like I am the object of scrutiny or that I have to "play act" for others anymore either. When I get difficult or strange symptoms, I now just slow down and focus on my breathing and that helps me a lot, along with my medication therapy.

I still remember very clearly how desperate and afraid I was when I first began going to Mental Health . There were a lot of times when I felt really terrified. After I had become really comfortable with my first tall therapist, she transferred to a different clinic and I got a new therapist who was a "tom-boy" type. My new tom-boy therapist also scared me at first, because I was not expecting her to *emphatically reject* the façade that I sometimes tried to use in order to impress other people. My initial complaint was that she just really didn't like the "pretty girl" I had been trying to convey for so long, the way I thought both my tall therapist and my father did. In truth, that was never me and I had only used that facade for my own "survival" identity at the time – it was a desperate attempt to escape "The Face". Looking back, I realize now that my own mother didn't approve of that contrived *façade* identity either. My tom-boy therapist would become the counselor I would have for most of my "healing" years and she was very influential for me. I only began to accept and step away from the contrived façade and from my other desperate reactions to relentless ongoing symptoms because of her. I don't feel so desperate anymore.

Over the years, I now have learned to live and function without a façade. I have also been able to emotionally survive, in a different and perhaps more comfortable way, due to effective, regular medication and to my tomboy therapist's therapeutic support. I became really close to her after almost two years into therapy and began to also trust and respect her. Eventually, I would become able to appreciate her *a whole lot,* but it took a while. After three years of seeing her, I finally felt it was time to unveil to her what I had been afraid to tell anyone else at the clinic. This was the formerly hidden secret about my broadcasting. This took a lot of courage for me to admit to her or to anyone else because a part of me really believed my broadcasting and extra-sensory powers were *real* at the time!

My tom-boy therapist had always handled my admissions calmly, and when I told her about this, she just referred to my *"power"* as a "symptom". She would always remind me of that when I had similar delusions of grandeur - that "I was just having *symptoms*." She would always keep that reality on my mind and, at the beginning of each session, she would ask me, "... and the symptoms? ... how are the *symptoms*? ... I had my "Tom boy" therapist for a total of six years. She was both meek and soft spoken but she could also be tough. She would later transfer to the Department of Rehabilitation where she is still helping others today. I met with her briefly in 2005 at a vegetarian sandwich shop and we shared common interests and camaraderie that day, together, just like "two old friends".

I was also treated by my first prescribing psychiatrist for ten full years before he left the area. He had always helped with medication adjustments and guided me, once warning me about drug interactions such as diet pills or herbal supplements that should not be used with my medication. He even wanted to lend me a really nice beautiful big book on Van Gogh, but he teased me, saying it would be "too heavy for me to carry". I really felt in a way, at peace with his humor but it would have definitely bothered me in the past. I miss the special support that he gave me which was very different and more unique than any other psychiatrist's support has been. I am lucky and should be very thankful to have had a few good father figures in my life such as that psychiatrist, my job coach, George, and my handsome new neighbor in addition to the limited time I spent with my own real, biological father. I think it has realistically taken an army of men to help me overcome the devastating absence of my father when I was a child growing up - it was so painful for me.

142

I would also be lucky that my second prescribing psychiatrist was another tall, attractive, enthusiastic woman who, surprisingly, I felt really comfortable around. I had her for five peaceful, productive years during the time I was still working at the key shop. She was proud of my accomplishments and listened attentively to all of my adventures at work. She always told me I could take less of my medication when I would complain about it or even would suggest that I take a really small extra dose of my medication before driving my long anxious drive from Ventura to Oxnard to see her. Although she was very special in her own way too, just like my boss was at the time, she also had a way, as all psychiatrists do, of keeping a certain "professional" distance from me. I have now come to expect this from any psychiatrist. It was also a little unsettling for me at first, but I have learned that psychiatrists are human beings too. On occasion, I have even had to use some form of "self-talk" in order to resist my own initial interpretation of a doctor's comment or reaction that might otherwise make me feel suspicious or uncomfortable. They are human and their own effect on me can sometimes be unintentional.

I felt very fortunate to have my "Tall Therapist." When she was about to be transferred to another clinic, I expressed my fears about talking to someone else and having to go through getting to know a new doctor again. After I told her how afraid I was that he or she might not really understand my condition, she even called me at home later to comfort me. She told me not to worry so much and assured me it would all be fine by building my confidence and faith in the future. She simply said to me to keep one important reality in the forefront of my mind - "You *know what you have* now."

My last, most recent, therapist who I will call my "Authentic" therapist really helped me to assert myself in another new really tough situation I would later find myself in. She was wonderful, down-to earth and didn't care much for any "attitudes" either. I was so afraid of people's reactions to me, but my "Authentic therapist" told me that when asserting yourself, "it shows that you care." I had never before in my life ever thought of speaking up for myself in that way. When I had symptoms and felt as though I was losing my way, she also continually reminded me to use "self-talk" and to breathe correctly as a means of comforting myself. Remembering to do these important things, when you need to, can be easy to forget sometimes. She once even shared with me that she believed what we see on television was not "real" life and that people should not compare themselves to the actors they see on the screen. That is why I call her my "Authentic Therapist" and I agreed with her about that.

I immediately felt close to my "Authentic Therapist" right from the start. She was light-hearted and funny and even seemed to really enjoy my company more than any other therapist or psychiatrist had done in the past. Like my first psychiatrist, she also eventually retired after I only been with her for four years. This time, more than at any other time since I began therapy, I felt very disappointed. She told me that we would still remain together in our thoughts when I told her I would miss her.

My third, and now current prescribing psychiatrist, has been extremely "hands on". More than any other psychiatrist at this time, she seems more truly interested in my life than the other psychiatrists were. She also wants to help me a lot more than the others did which I truly appreciate. I shared with her that I was having trouble going to my apartment mailbox and sometimes even just sitting in my apartment and also seriously affected by the sound of slamming car doors. I even started having difficulty just going to Mental Health. In response, she prescribed me two more medications: Abilify for psychosis and Zoloft for obsessive thoughts. She had also lowered my nightly dosage of Zyprexa. These adjustments have helped me engage more actively in life and to become less fearful. I have discovered that Abilify has almost no side effects, which are common with the newer medications and it also allows me a little more of the excitement and energy I experienced and enjoyed during my younger years. Thankfully, my other lurking fears and beliefs, such as my broadcasting delusions do not seem so real to me anymore because of the addition of Zoloft to my treatment regimen.

Looking back now, I can see and recognize all of those delusions and false perceptions - and even the reasons why "The FACE" was such a troubling disaster. My mental problems were always, from the very early beginning, biologically and genetically based. I could not avoid experiencing the symptoms I had and should not blame myself or others - nor should I be blamed *by* others for having them. They are also not simply "mind over matter" problems like I used to think they were. Once I finally started my medication, after fighting against taking it for so long - I could begin to stop running away from other people and even from my own "self" in total terror. Without professional help, my mind, during those early days, was very slowly degrading - and I definitely could have ended up homeless, like my grandmother did, if I would had taken the wrong path. I still have a strong hunch that maybe some significant symptoms were even present in my early childhood nightmares and imaginings. It's hard to really know for sure.

Therapy, doctors, medication, and everyday life are all getting better for me, not worse. My three different therapists have all been helpful in different ways. Therapists can be wonderful, just like psychiatrists are, but they are even better when you can feel close to them. Today, I still fight back the fear of ever having to get a new psychiatrist again and, even worse, of ever being accused of taking the "easy way out" by one of them because I am no longer working at my old job. It is still very hard for me today, any time I am forced to go and see someone new at mental health, but I have been lucky in these situations, both with therapists and with psychiatrists, since I have often had to see both, as part of my treatment.

I also feel much more normal now and I don't sabotage the medications I have been prescribed with caffeine, sugar, and nicotine like I did in the past anymore. I now feel more of a positive effect from the medication, itself, and don't feel the caffeine and sugar is as necessary. I am still an off and on smoker, but have also managed to reduce those to almost nothing. "Schizophrenia Symptoms Causes Treatments"[48] is a very informative book I read once that I highly recommend to others. It does a really good job of describing the fear and guilt that I often had. It also helped me to define myself as a person and begin to better understand why I once felt so worthless. In this book, one patient described his feelings about being a fraud,

"In my life, in my personality, there is an essence of falseness and insincerity. A thin vapor of fraud hangs always over me and dampens and injures some things in me that I value."[49]

Due to my needed medications, adjustments, and obsessing too much, I probably also will have a lifelong sometimes disabling difficulty with poor concentration. I keep trying to communicate to people and explain the things I can no longer do because of these limitations. I am, at the same time, able to focus much better on creative projects now and I also believe in persistence. I still continue to keep trying to concentrate better, keep up with my daily responsibilities regularly - and I never, never give up on myself. My authentic therapist reminded me once that the mind needs to rest sometimes, so I do also try to seek out a quiet time alone on occasion. When I do that, although rarely, I can escape for a few moments from all of my problems, worries and even from the creative ideas that are always continuously entering my mind.

I am also more grateful now for both my mother and my father. My father guided me during my childhood years and my

---

[48] Bernheim, Lewine, Schizophrenia, Symptoms Causes Treatments; W.W. Norton & Company Inc. 1979

[49] Bernheim, Lewine. Schizophrenia Symptoms Causes Treatments" p. 49. W.W. Norton & Company Inc. 1979

mother did so then as well as during and after my diagnosis. I'm lucky to have had parents who really loved me and I try to live up to their aspirations for me. I also try to maintain that same spirit that they both recognized in me from the very beginning, even when my mother was still pregnant with me. I hope that I can live up to the special, very original middle name, "Elanne", my parents gave me. It is a unique feminine "variation" they created together from the French word "elan" ("elan vitale" meaning life force). That phrase was used frequently by my very philosophical father about my mother during his many early conversations with her, so I feel his voice and her spirited energy lives through me – even though he is now gone from this earth.

I don't regret missed opportunities much although I do believe I may have been diagnosed and treated for my illness a little late. As much as I loved him and still do, I finally had to stop listening to my father's advice about Scientology as the only answer for my disorder. I have now accepted my diagnosis (at least somewhat) and have decided to keep living my life the way I am living it right now. It is still never completely easy for me to do - and Scientology still calls me on the telephone sometimes hoping for another recruit. It seems that I am also never functioning correctly without being able to do my art. Art is my only real, everyday therapy right now. I also still maintain hope that someday I may be able to support myself without relying on help from social security for my ongoing disability. That is my dream.

Maybe someday I'll get a full time job in a totally different new and exciting place or make a whole lot of money with my creative endeavors. Now I feel a lot more is possible. My "authentic" therapist once told me that, yes, I could try moving to a new city, but that I would probably would be facing the same, exact problems there that I am facing now and I have to realize that her jest could be right. I currently see my "hands on" psychiatrist every two months and feel that this treatment plan is ideal for me. Recently, while I was being evaluated by a case worker, he commented "Wow! You've been seeing mental health for a *long time!*" Indeed, time *has really gone by quickly* for me, as the years go by, but I have never thought of it that way.

I have now come to acknowledge and to better understand my own maternal grandmother's paranoid schizophrenic illness and I also recognize the ordeal faced by all of the other individuals who have struggled with this mysterious and very serious illness – *one that I also have* – just like them. I also think about all of the people living now that still struggle or are just beginning their own battle like I did, long ago. I wonder ...

"Where are they now?"..."Are they afraid?"..."Did they become homeless?... "Or did they end up resorting to violence?" ... "Are they receiving any help?"..."Do they ever feel loved?"..."Why does the road turn this way for some of us ... ?"

I consider myself very lucky that I have made some very difficult - but good decisions along the way. Another very informative book, written by a top expert in the field, I once read called, "Surviving Schizophrenia"[50] states that schizophrenics, as a group, don't tend to live very long. I genuinely hope to prove that statistic wrong and live a long, healthy, life. I have also tried to make amends with others from my difficult past whenever possible. My old boyfriend Russell and I even met for a brief amount of time at a coffee shop, once, and I am at peace with him now. Russell told me that he had developed a love for sailing and four-wheeling, and later asked me, "Isn't it easier for you now - knowing what you have?" My answer to him was "Definitely, Yes!"

My former high school love, "Sweetheart", now has two children and he seems to be very happy. My former admirer and roommate "Red" went back to live in his hometown Alabama and my once amicable best girlfriend, Shelley, now has a

---

[50] Torrey, E. Fuller (2001)

beautiful little boy. I am sure she is an exceptional mother. I have also given up going to see "Adonis" after seeing him in concert six times, but I am very thankful that I had him for my "fantasy love" and "rock star" in the past. He is now still, a passing thought sometimes and he is still busy making great music.

I now do art on a more regular basis and hope that many will someday enjoy my work. I am proud and grateful to say that my artwork has been featured three times in magazines that are published to raise funds for brain research to understand more about and help the mentally ill. Three of my original paintings are also hanging on the walls at my mental health clinic. I am also happy to have also written, illustrated, and published a total of eight books. Almost all of these are children's books, authored in my own name.[51] I decided, long ago, not to have children of my own, due to the possible prenatal side effects attributed to my medication, so my children's books are my gift to *all children!* My love of children and of animals are celebrated joyously in the pages of my books and I hope that the children and parents who read them enjoy this as much as I enjoyed writing them. When I think about how my writing my own books began to happen, I remember my authentic therapist the most - the one who I stress again, enjoyed being with me more so than all of the others seemed to. I think of her a lot.

I also think of the friendship my mother and I have had and about her optimistic assistance and help. Every day in my life now seems so different to me than the last one and my mother has been my best friend throughout all of this. Her smile lights my darkest corners. She and I have gone out to many restaurants, have shopped together, and   become even closer now that we sometimes work together on artistic projects. Her own editing skills were helpful to me when I was writing this book. She now lives farther away from me, but we talk on the phone often, and communicate with each other by email

---

[51] See Appendix and About the Author sections in the book for more details.

frequently.

My handsome neighbor and I have also become great friends and close partners now. We are happy when we are together and I am thankful for the positive communication we both share. I have always loved animals - to the ends of the earth - and I now have two wonderful cats who actually think they are dogs – along with two lovebirds that always sing praises - and even get along with the cats!

I have also, recently, become even more fascinated by my schizophrenic grandmother "Lily" who I never knew. I have heard a lot about her brave, fun-loving, "free-spirit" personality despite the torture in her life before she disappeared and I always want to see new photos of the woman I share so much in common with.

Although nobody knows what eventually happened to Lily, I am sure she is in heaven now, in a place of real authority. I have candles at home now... and they are lit as a silent prayer for her ...

Lily 1938

Candle   2016

The End

"Having Faith"   2016

Poems/
Echoes

A Child

A child knows
right from wrong
without being
taught.
We are born
to be
something
more with
god's blessings.

Exhilaration

I feel happy now
strange it seems
others are cautious
or even angry!
Exhilaration feels
like I am free
My labors have
proved fruitless
a mystery to me
why do I feel
exhilaration?

Social Graces

My mental
makeup has
caused a loss of
social graces
I have made
friends
with those
'other voices'
 it's hard to go
 to many places
 because
 of my choices

The Condition...

It's unbelievable that
things could seem
this bad
swimming in a sea
of drugs
crawling and scratching
I want to believe
in spectacular things
how could my brain
have taken
these wings

Assertiveness

Assertiveness can
mean a
show of care

My mind reeling ...

I won't act on cue

I won't feel it
is a kind act

because I can't.

Accepted

What a glory
to be accepted
even though
painfully I
fight these
struggles
I appreciate
the attempts
of others...
and being
part of
this
kingdom

..

Open the door...

Never ask for much
Be grateful
for what you are given
Be generous
with what you have
even if you have very little
Listen to others
even if you do not
agree with them
Forgive friends and
enemies
Be content with what
you have and yourself
Envy no one
Be respectful regardless
of race
Help the elderly
may we all live that
long...

Open the door.. E.R.G 2005

In this world
today...
I could not
exist without
animals...
Animals do not judge...
Animals respond to
love
habitually
loyally

Alone
I am alone
even with company
satiated by my medication
I can sing as long
as there is
something to
do
sometimes I am
crazy for
stopping so soon
The voices ended it

Happy to have a mom

What a blessing
 to have a mom
She shows me who I am
With gentle words she
guides
more meaningful as
time passes
So lucky I am!
And lucky are
the girls who have
a mom!

Dreams ...

are the ruler of
all things..
from sleep
a reason to
awake!
from apathy
to now
consider..
It is
conceived
that
without
dreams..
you have
no
wings.

Famous ...

I want to be
Famous
If I were
I could build
a bridge
I can't stop the
insanity
but I could
try
This fire inside
is still mine
if there is still
hope for me
I will reach
to imagine...

The Sun

The sun is
too bright
it's a rude
awakening
shaking me and
telling me
you are not
right
my butterfly
wings gone
my mind
soon reminds
of a broken bond

"Inner world"

Sometimes I am
in a place
feeling helpless
look at me with
emotions I can't relate
at the moment
you have caused
offense
conflicted
I will
surrender
to my inner
world.

Titles of art in poetry section:

"In the Garden" 2016
"Listening" 1987
"Lonely Waters" (crane) 2007
"Baby Mountain Lion" 1995
"Ocean Waves" 2012
" Mums" 2007
"Vibrant Daisies" 2005
"Rose Parchment" 2011

Angel Cat (2016)

. . . This book is also dedicated
to cats who mean so much . . .

CITINGS

Schizophrenia, Symptoms Causes Treatments; Berheim, Lewine, W.W. Norton & Company Inc. 1979,

Surviving Schizophrenia, E. Fuller Torrey, Quill Harper Collins Publishers 2001

Schizophrenia Origins, Processes, Treatment, and Outcome Oxford University Press Inc. Cromwell, Snyder 1993

Experience of Schizophrenia, Michael Robbins, The Guilford Press 1993

Oxford Journals of Schizophrenia; Mandal, Pandey, Prasad University of Maryland School of Medicine 1998

The British American Journal; Palala Press, British Medical Asssociation(creator) 2015

Encyclopedia and Dictionary of Medicine Nursing and Allied Health Saunders (7th edition) Miller- Keene , O Toole 2005

The Anger Trap; Dr. Les Carter, Jossey-Bass A Wiley Imprint 2004

The Power of Positive Thinking; Dr. Norman Vincent Peale, Fireside Rockefeller Center 2003

Webster's New World Dictionary; Simon & Schuster Inc. 1990

WebMd, http://www.webmd.com 2005-2016

Newsweek Magazine Online http://www.newsweek.com 2015

The Scientology Handbook L. Ron Hubbard Bridge Pub. 1994

How to Choose your People; Hubbard, Minshull Ann Arbor 1972

Awake! Magazine Church of Scientology International L. Ron Hubbard 2005

Jennifer Walker, whose pen
name is Stella Grey, lives
in California with her four
cats. She enjoys writing and
illustrating children's books
and painting. You can find
her books on amazon.com.

See more!

www.kindkidsbooks.com

www.ingramcontent.com/pod-product-compliance
Lightning Source LLC
Chambersburg PA
CBHW062003280526
45787CB00005B/1976